Anonymous

Mohawk Valley Cook Book

Anonymous

Mohawk Valley Cook Book

ISBN/EAN: 9783744781268

Printed in Europe, USA, Canada, Australia, Japan

Cover: Foto ©Lupo / pixelio.de

More available books at **www.hansebooks.com**

MOHAWK VALLEY COOK BOOK.

Compiled and Published

—BY—

THE LADIES' SOCIETY

—OF—

ST. MARK'S LUTHERAN CHURCH,

CANAJOHARIE, N. Y.

1889.

FIRST EDITION.

A copy of this Cook Book will be mailed to any address on receipt of Fifty cents. Apply to

MRS. BENJAMIN SMITH, Sec'y.

1889.
PRESS OF L. C. CHILDS & SON,
UTICA, N. Y.

COPYRIGHT, 1889.

PREFACE.

"*She looketh well to the ways of her household.*"

The MOHAWK VALLEY COOK BOOK has been prepared and carefully revised with special reference to the needs of young and inexperienced housekeepers; great pains have been taken to write out each recipe clearly, so that if followed closely, success will be certain; and *all have been thoroughly tested and proved to be valuable.* Much of the information which it contains will be found useful in every home, of which the "house-mother" is herself the head; to these and all, the contents of this little book are commended by

THE LADIES OF ST. MARK'S LUTHERAN CHURCH,

Canajoharie, N. Y.

SOUPS.

GENERAL DIRECTIONS.

In making soups of almost every kind, it is absolutely necessary to wash the meat thoroughly before putting it into the kettle, with plenty of cold water to cover it. For a general rule, allow one quart of water to one pound of meat; set it on the range or stove where it will heat slowly, and as soon as the scum begins to rise, stand with skimmer in hand, and take it carefully off, until no more appears. Should the water boil too violently, throw in half a cup of cold water, and turn the meat over in the kettle, when the rest of the scum will be disengaged and float to the top. When this is done, set the kettle where it will simmer slowly for at least four hours, not adding any salt until nearly done. If the soup is wanted for use the same day, it should now be strained through a colander, the fat skimmed off, and allowed to settle for a few minutes, when it can be returned to the kettle, to add whatever ingredients or seasoning may be desired. The juices of the meat will be best extracted, if it is cut in small pieces, and the larger bones crushed, before putting into water. It is better, if possible, to make the soup or stock the day before it is wanted, strain it, and set it aside in a bright tin pan, or large earthen bowl; when cold, the fat will lift off easily, before putting it on the stove, and it can be poured off carefully, so as not to disturb the settlings. Should a perfectly clear broth be desired, it can be strained again, (after heating, if the soup has jellied) through a bag, which has first been wrung out of hot water. Cheese cloth, doubled, makes the softest and most suitable straining bag for this purpose.

The meat of beef shank makes a standard soup,—veal or mutton added to this give additional flavor to it; or these can be used alone. The trimmings of large roasts, of chops, steak, etc., can all be used to make delicious broths, taken raw, or after having been upon the table, and the bones and less choice portions of fowls,—turkey, chicken or duck, can be saved for the same purpose. These cooked meats should be thoroughly washed in scalding water, to remove all taste of gravy or dressing, then put into the kettle with plenty of cold water, skimming if necessary, and proceeding according to former directions. Should the soup boil down too much, hot water can be added at any time after skimming.

A half-cup of rice is sufficient for from three to four quarts of soup. It should be well washed, and boiled in the broth for at least half an an hour; the same quantity of sago is needed, but will boil in half the time. If herbs are used for flavoring, they should be tied in small bunches if fresh, or in a small piece of soft cloth if dried. If not wanted for immediate use, the soup or stock will keep for several days, if set away in a very cool place.

VEGETABLE SOUP.

To three quarts of stock, add a large handful of cabbage cut very fine, three large potatoes cut into dice, half a pint of tomatoes, one or more onions, as desired, also cut fine; carrots in small pieces can be added, and all boiled for half an hour, or longer, until vegetables are thoroughly cooked. If you wish thickening, beat together one egg, one heaped teaspoon of flour, and two tablespoonfuls of milk, and add it to the soup a few minutes before serving. It is well to stir gradually into this mixture of milk, egg and flour, a little of the hot broth; then return all to the kettle, stirring the soup, as it is poured in, to prevent curdling.

ASPARAGUS SOUP.

Take about seventy heads of asparagus, cut away the hard parts, and boil the rest until tender. Throw half of it into cold water; press the rest through a sieve, or fine colander, and stir it into three pints of stock; add salt, pepper, a teaspoon of sugar, and let all come to a boil; cut the remaining asparagus into small pieces, put them into the soup, let it boil up, and then it is ready to serve.

FROM "50 SOUPS."

TRY PRESERVING YOUR FRUIT WITHOUT HEAT.

MACARONI SOUP.

Break one-third of a pound of macaroni into small (two inch) pieces; boil for half an hour, or until soft, in slightly salted water, then drain. Have about two quarts of stock, boiling hot; add the cooked macaroni; season with salt and white pepper; boil a moment, and serve.

VERMICELLI SOUP.

Boil in stock—beef or mutton—two tablespoonfuls finely minced celery to one quart; when tender, and about five minutes before taking up, stir in two tablespoonfuls of vermicelli, broken into pieces.

BLACK BEAN SOUP.

Soak one pint and a half of black beans in water over night; put them over the next morning to cook, in plenty of cold water, adding more as it boils away; in four hours, and perhaps sooner, they will be soft enough to mash through a colander; stir them gradually into two quarts of boiling stock, with half a pint of cooked tomatoes, which have previously been put through a colander; mix a tablespoon of flour, very smooth, with a little water, and stir into the soup just before taking up; slice about half a lemon into the tureen just before serving.   MRS. EMELINE F. SMITH.

WHITE BEAN SOUP.

This can be made in the same way, omitting the tomatoes and the sliced lemon.

POTATO SOUP.

Three medium sized potatoes, 1 pint sweet milk, 1 teaspoon of chopped onion, 1 teaspoon each of chopped celery and parsley. (The latter two may be omitted.) One tablespoon of butter, rubbed with ½ tablespoon of flour, and cooked in ½ pint of boiling milk. Boil the potatoes in salted water, until quite soft, and boil the onion, celery and parsley in the pint of milk. When potatoes are cooked, drain and mash them, and pour over them the boiling milk, stirring fast. Put through a fine strainer, rubbing as much of the potato through as possible,—set on the stove to boil, adding salt, pepper and a little cayenne, and when boiling, stir in the flour and butter thickened in the cup of milk. Strain into the tureen immediately. This is sufficient for six.

MRS. J. C. M'CLURE.

TOMATO SOUP, WITHOUT MEAT.

One quart of stewed tomatoes, either fresh or canned, one quart boiling water. When heated thoroughly, put through a sieve or fine strainer, so as to make perfectly smooth ; stir in a half teaspoon of soda, and one pint sweet milk ; season with salt, pepper and a teaspoon of butter. Stir well, and serve immediately.

BOUILLON.

Is a very strong, clear beef broth. When done, it must be allowed to cool, when the whole of the fat should be removed. When wanted for use, it must be strained, seasoned with salt and pepper, and served very hot. If other flavoring is desired, of herbs, summer savory, sweet basil, majoram, etc., they should be boiled for a short time in the broth, before straining.

BREAD-DICE FOR SOUP.

Cut rather dry bread into small squares, and fry in very hot butter until brown, not burned. Put into the tureen, and pour the boiling stock of beef, veal or chicken over it.

CHICKEN SOUP.

Cut up one chicken, and put it into the soup-kettle with two quarts of cold water ; skim and boil slowly for more than an hour. Add then, one teaspoon of salt and a very little pepper, and two desert spoonfuls of washed rice ; boil half an hour longer, add a gill of cream, or a half pint of milk, and serve as soon as boiling, having taken out the chicken. A part of this, if desired, may be cut in small pieces, and returned to the soup.

TRY PRESERVING YOUR FRUIT WITHOUT HEAT.

MOCK BISQUE SOUP.

One quart can tomato, 3 pints milk, 1 large tablespoon flour, butter the size of an egg, pepper and salt to taste, 1 scant teaspoon of soda. Put the tomato over to stew, reserve a half cup of milk, with which mix the flour smoothly, and put the rest over in a double kettle to boil ; stir in the mixed flour and milk, and boil ten minutes longer. To the tomato add the soda, stirring well, and rub through a sieve, or a strainer that is fine enough to keep back the seeds ; add butter, salt and pepper to the milk, then the tomatoes, and serve immediately. If half the portion is made, stir the tomato in the can well before dividing. * * *

MRS. M. L. SMITH.

GREEN CORN SOUP.

Six large ears of green corn, grate the corn from the cobs, and scrape them. Put the cobs in a kettle, and cover them with boiling water ; boil from fifteen to twenty minutes, remove the cobs, add the grated corn, and enough sweet milk to make a quart, or a little more. Add butter, salt and pepper, boil ten minutes and serve.

MRS. S. A. READ.

TOMATO CREAM SOUP, NO. 2.

Cut up six ripe tomatoes, and put them over to stew ; boil one pint of milk in a double boiler, mix two large teaspoonfuls of flour, with a very little milk till smooth, then stir it into the boiling milk ; cook ten minutes. To the tomato put one scant salt spoon of soda, stir well, rub through a strainer fine enough to keep back seeds ; add a desert spoonful of butter to the milk, stirring well, then the tomato, and serve immediately. * * *

MRS. M. L. S.

CLEAR SOUP.

Three lbs soup meat, or a soup bone weighing that : gash the meat well, and put it on to cook with three quarts of cold water, three teaspoons of salt, half a one of pepper,—one small carrot, one turnip, one large onion, (each should weigh 3 oz. after peeling,) stick one clove in the onion ; cut the vegetables, and add them to the meat,

---

USING PETTIT'S CIDER AND FRUIT PRESERVATIVE.

after it has boiled slowly two hours, then boil three hours more, so slowly that just an occasional bubble comes to the surface. The soup must have been skimmed when it first came to the boil, according to the previous directions for soup; it must be skimmed again after the vegetables are in. When done, strain, then set away to cool; take off the fat, and pour very carefully through a clean cloth, keeping the sediment, which can be used for gravy. This should make two quarts and a pint of clear soup, if the boiling has been very slow, and the kettle kept covered.

MRS. M. L. S.

TOMATO SOUP NO. 3.

Take one quart stewed tomatoes, either canned or fresh, heat and put through a fine colander, or a strainer which will retain the seeds; then add to two quarts strong soup-stock, seasoning with salt and pepper to taste. Add a teaspoonful of butter, and a little celery salt.

MRS. J. C. M'C

NOODLES FOR SOUP.

Break two eggs into flour, with three tablespoonfuls warm water, and a pinch of salt. Mix to a very stiff paste, roll *very* thin; rub flour over the surface, and cut in four inch strips; lay them in a pile, and with a sharp knife cut as fine as possible. When soup is done, drop in, and boil ten minutes.

MOCK TURTLE SOUP.

Soak one pint of turtle soup-bean in cold water over night. In the morning put over to boil (in fresh water), one hour before putting in the meat, about three lbs., for which veal is best; add salt and pepper, three or four whole cloves, the same of allspice, and a little sweet marjoram, if you have it. Boil till beans are very soft and mash through a colander, all except the skins and spice. Put back into the kettle to keep hot; cut a few nice pieces of the meat the size of a filbert, a half lemon sliced very fine, peel and all; two hard boiled eggs sliced and put in the tureen. Pour the boiling soup over all, and serve. The meat may be left out.

MRS. D. S. R.

TRY PRESERVING YOUR FRUIT WITHOUT HEAT,

MEATS, POULTRY, &C.

OF BEEF.

The middle ribs and sirloin are best for roasting. A piece of ten lbs. will require about three hours roasting; one of from four to six lbs. will cook easily in an hour and a half, unless it is desired to be thoroughly done; but any amount of time beyond this specified, only serves to make the meat more dry. Mutton also is liked a little underdone by many; but veal, lamb and pork must be well-cooked, and are better over, rather than underdone. Poultry also must be well cooked, whether roasted or fricasseed. A large turkey (10 to 12 lbs.) will take from three to three and a half hours to roast; fowls of medium size from one and a half to two hours. To boil meats or poultry, put them into hot water, moderately salted, remove scum as it rises, and let them boil slowly, until perfectly tender, but no longer. The time required varies with the size and toughness of that which is cooked; when a fork enters easily, it may be considered done.

BEEF, A la MODE.

Take a round roast of beef, weighing seven or eight lbs.; make a number of incisions in it, with a sharp knife, into which press strips of salt pork, four inches long, and half an inch each way in thickness. Season well with salt, pepper, cloves, allspice, cinnamon, a very little, and the same of nutmeg, all well mixed, and rubbed into the meat. Put into the pan with one pint hot water, and roast very slowly for at least two hours and a half, basting frequently, and adding to the water as it boils away. When nearly done, if desired, add $\frac{1}{2}$ pint of sherry wine to the gravy, and continue to baste. Take from the pan when done, and thicken the gravy remaining with a tablespoon of flour, mixed to a cream with cold water. Boil up for five minutes, and turn into gravy bowl.

BEEF STEAK,

That from the round is most generally fried, after having been well pounded. Take about a tablespoon each of butter and fresh dripping; have it very hot in the pan, put in the steak, letting it brown quickly on one side, then turn it, cover up closely, and finish cooking. Take from pan on hot platter, turn a cupful of hot water into the pan, and thicken the gravy with a full teaspoon of flour, mixed with a little water. Boil up, pour over steak and serve.

BREF STEAK AND ONIONS.

Use for this round steak. About half an hour before cooking it, peel from one to two dozen onions, according to size, and put over to boil. When steak is done, drain the onions in a colander, cut them up, and put them in the frying pan, season with salt and pepper, dredge in a little flour, and add a tablespoonful of butter; stir well together, put in the pan over the fire, stirring often; when they are soft and a little brown, return the steak to the pan, and heat all together. Put the meat on a dish, pour the onions and gravy over it, and serve very hot.

STEAK FOR BROILING.

Use sirloin or porterhouse steak; broil over a brisk fire, on gridiron or in strong toaster; turn frequently; do not season until done. After being placed on the dish, place upon it small bits of butter, and stand in the oven for a minute. Or a gravy can be prepared with as much or as little butter as you wish to use, one gill hot water, a sprinkle of flour, salt and pepper; put into a pie-plate in a warm place, and when the steak is on the dish, pour over it.

STEWED KIDNEYS.

Take a pair of beef kidneys, free from fat and gristle; wash well, once in cold water, then in hot water. Cook for three or four hours, changing water each hour, doing this the day before, if wanted for breakfast next morning; cut them up in inch pieces, put over to stew in the water in which they were boiled; add salt pepper and butter to taste, thicken the gravy with a little flour, stirred up with cold water; serve as hot as possible.

TRY PRESERVING YOUR FRUIT WITHOUT HEAT.

MOCK DUCK.

Have a round steak cut half an inch thick; remove the bone, sewing up the holes. Make a dressing of about a cupful of bread crumbs, a teaspoonful of butter, a little chopped onion, pepper and salt, well mixed, spread on the meat; roll up and sew together, put in a kettle on top of range, cover very closely, and cook for three hours, turning often, and adding more water when needed. When done, remove the threads, place on a platter, thicken the gravy slightly, and pour over the meat.

SMOKED BEEF WITH CREAM.

Cut very thin, put into boiling water and cook a couple of minutes, turn off the water, and replace with rich sweet cream, letting it come to a boil, and season with pepper. If you have no cream, use milk, a teaspoon of butter, and thicken with a very little flour.

SMOKED BEEF, WITH EGGS.

Cut thin, and let stand a few minutes in boiling water. Heat a lump of butter, the size of a hickory nut in the frying pan; brown the beef in this, after turning off the water. Have ready some lightly beaten eggs, in number as desired, from two to six, pour into the hot beef, stir briskly until the eggs are cooked, and serve immediately.

ROAST VEAL.

The best for this purpose is from the loin, from five to eight pounds in weight. It will need one-third longer cooking than beef. If you have some of the flanky, thin part with the roast, make a dressing of bread crumbs softened with milk, a large teaspoon of butter, pepper, salt, and a little finely chopped onion, if desired; lay on the meat, fold over, and sew together, or bind around tightly with a cord. Baste often, having rubbed salt upon the meat before it is put in the pan, and sprinkle it lightly with pepper. If possible, serve grated horseradish to eat with it.

VEAL CUTLET.

Can be dipped in egg, then in fine bread crumbs, put into the pan in which some butter or dripping has been made very hot. Cover up tight, and cook slowly, turning when well browned.

VEAL CUTLET AND CHOPS.

Can be broiled as beefsteak, and are improved by small bits of butter put over the pieces before serving. They are excellent to have a large cup full of stewed tomatoes, very hot, poured upon the dish on which they are served.

VEAL LOAF.

Three and one-half pounds veal, fat and lean, and one-half pound salt pork, all chopped very fine. (It is better to have your butcher run it through the sausage-cutter.) Mix with six small crackers, rolled very fine, two eggs, butter the size of an egg (unless the meat is quite fat), one tablespoon salt, one grated nutmeg, one teaspoon black pepper, and a very small quantity of cayenne pepper. Mix thoroughly, and pack into a baking-pan; bake slowly, and baste often with the fat which will collect at the sides of the pan, or a little butter melted in hot water. When cool, slice very thin; garnish the dish with celery or parsley leaves.

MRS. C. G. PETTIT.

VEAL CROQUETTES.

Six coffee-cups of finely-chopped cooked veal. Put into a saucepan half a cup of butter, eight even tablespoons of flour; when they melt to a smooth paste, add three teacups of milk, a very small onion chopped fine, and two tablespoons of chopped parsley, and boil until thick. Turn into a bowl, and add three eggs, the chopped meat, and salt and pepper to taste; mix well, and set away to cool, when mold into oblong shape, dip in beaten egg, roll in bread or cracker crumbs, and boil a few minutes in hot lard. This makes 36 croquettes. They can be set away, and heated in the oven when wanted. CONTRIBUTED.

TRY PRESERVING YOUR FRUIT WITHOUT HEAT.

VEAL POT-PIE.

Take three pounds of the loin, cut in pieces and wash. Put in kettle with six strips of sweet salt pork, as large as one's middle finger, season with salt and pepper, cover with hot water, and set it stewing. Make a dough of one quart sifted flour, four teaspoons baking powder, rubbed together with butter the size of a small egg, and enough sweet milk stirred into it with a spoon to make it like biscuit dough. Let your veal stew half an hour or more, add boiling water till a little more than well covered, and set on top of stove where it will boil gently. Take a spoonful of dough at a time and lay over the top, cover with a tight cover so that no steam will escape. Listen to bubbling and keep it slowly boiling for 25 minutes, but do not uncover till done, when you ought to find a white fluffy mass. Dish the crust carefully, putting it around the edge of a large platter, the meat in the center. Over the whole pour the gravy. Should there not be enough broth left in the kettle, add a cup of hot water, butter the size of an egg, and flour to thicken. A cup of sweet cream is an addition.

MRS. S. A. R.

OR, VEAL POT-PIE NO. 2.

Cook the veal until done, making the gravy as directed above. Have the biscuit dough baked as biscuit, split open, lay on platter and lay meat on top, pouring the gravy over all, using milk to make it if you have no cream.

MRS. E. F. S.

VEAL LIVER.

Cut in slices about half an inch thick, wash well and dry on towel, roll in flour and fry till thoroughly done in a small quantity of dripping with a very little butter. When done, take up, turn a few tablespoons of hot water into the frying pan, shake it around and pour over the liver. That which remains of this or the uncooked liver, can be cut in pieces about two inches long and stewed till tender in a little hot water. When cooked, turn off the water, put over it sufficient milk to cover and a large teaspoonful of but-

USING PETTIT'S CIDER AND FRUIT PRESERVATIVE.

ter, thicken with a spoonful of flour, boil up a few minutes and serve.

MRS. E. F. S.

SWEETBREADS.

Wash in salted water, remove stringy parts, parboil fifteen minutes, slice in two, dip in egg and roll in bread or cracker crumbs; season and fry in hot lard.

SWEET-BREADS, FRICASSEED.

The cooked sweet-breads can be used, cutting them into small pieces and stewing for ten minutes in a little soup-stock or water, season with pepper and salt, add a teaspoon of butter and thicken the gravy with a little flour. If they are fresh, cut in thin slices, wash and cook for half an hour in water or soup-stock; then make gravy as before directed, adding, if desired, a half-cup cream and one well-beaten egg.

ESCALLOPED MEAT.

One pint minced meat, one teacupful dried bread crumbs, one tablespoon of butter, one egg, salt and pepper to taste. Mix together and add gravy, stock or milk to make the mass quite moist. Bake in an earthen dish one hour in a slow oven.

VEAL KIDNEYS, STEWED.

Soak in cold salt water for several hours (if for breakfast, over night.) Boil fifteen minutes, pour off first water and boil in another till tender. Cut the kidneys into small pieces, and with the broth make a gravy, thickening slightly with flour, and adding milk, salt and pepper. Spices and wine can be added if desired.

MISS L. C. BAUM.

BAKED VEAL OR CHICKEN POT PIE.

Line the sides of a small dinner pot with pie crust. Take from two to three pounds of veal or chicken, cut in small pieces and place in the pot with alternate layers of sliced potatoes until pot is full; seasoning the layers as they are put in, with salt, pepper and

TRY PRESERVING YOUR FRUIT WITHOUT HEAT.

small pieces of butter, filling in with hot water sufficient to cook the meat and leave enough for a gravy. Lay over the whole a cover of pie crust, in the center of which cut a small slit. Cover loosely, set on top of stove, and cook very slowly for two hours; then uncover and put in the oven for half an hour. Take off the top crust, thicken the gravy, put it and the meat and side crust on the platter, laying the top crust over all.

ROAST LAMB.

Young lamb should be thoroughly roasted and brought to the table with a browned gravy made in the pan in which it has been cooked, and with mint sauce made thus :

MINT SAUCE.

Take fresh young mint, wash and dry on cloth, chop very fine; take of it three heaped tablespoons and mix with two of sugar. After fifteen minutes pour over it about half a cup of good but not too strong vinegar.

LAMB CHOPS,

As well as mutton chops, must be broiled. Lamb cutlets can be either fried or broiled; if fried, a brown gravy can be made by putting a little hot water in frying-pan after meat has been taken out, letting it boil up, and thickening with flour.

RAGOUT OF LAMB.

Take from the neck or breast of lamb about one pound and a half and cut in small pieces. In a frying pan put a tablespoon of butter and one of flour: set on the stove until melted and a pale brown, stirring slowly all the time. Pare and slice one onion and one carrot, and add to this brownish paste or *roux ;* also one pint of peas if desired, and the meat, seasoning with salt and pepper, and also a teaspoon of vinegar. Stir well together and put on close cover, cook slowly and be careful that it does not burn. After cooking twenty minutes add two-thirds pint of hot water and a little parsley, cover again closely and set where it will just simmer and cook until meat is tender. "CATHARINE OWEN."

USING PETTIT'S CIDER AND FRUIT PRESERVATIVE.

BOILED MUTTON.

Take a leg of mutton, wash it well and put it into boiling salted water, and boil from two to three hours, according to size. Serve it with plain drawn butter or with caper sauce. Make these sauces as follows: Drawn Butter—Mix well together two teaspoons of flour and two ounces butter. (Butter the size of a small egg will be two ounces.) When well mixed, pour gradually into it one pint boiling water, stirring all the time, and then set on the stove, and continue to stir until it just comes to a boil, when it is done. This sauce can also be made with milk. For Caper Sauce—Add two large tablespoons of capers just before serving.

MRS. E. F. SMITH.

MUTTON CHOPS.

Season with salt and pepper and broil slowly till thoroughly done.

PORK.

In cooking pork, it should be slowly done, and care should be taken that it is thoroughly cooked.

TO BOIL A HAM.

Wash and clean perfectly in two or three warm waters; put it into a large pot with cold water enough to cover; let it come to a boil, then set on the back part of the stove, and cook slowly till done throughout. A ham of twelve pounds will take about six hours to cook. Fill in as the water boils away, or else the ham will be too salt, and try with a fork towards the last, which will pierce easily when it is cooked enough. Take up, skin, and trim away dark spots; stick a clove here and there into the fat surface, or put little spots of black pepper instead.

HAM PATTIES.

Chop fine some scraps of lean boiled ham, and mix with an equal amount of crumbed bread, seasoning with pepper. A tablespoon of butter, or the like quantity of the fat, chopped, can be added. Moisten with milk to a soft paste. Fill muffin tins with

---

TRY PRESERVING YOUR FRUIT WITHOUT HEAT.

the mixture, and break an egg on top of each, sprinkling over them salt, pepper, and a few cracker or bread crumbs. Put in the oven and bake ten minutes, or until the eggs are cooked.

CONTRIBUTED.

TO CORN BEEF.

Make a brine that will bear up an egg, showing a spot as large as a "nickel." Heat and skim till clear, and pour hot over the beef, adding two ounces salt petre to a quarter of the beef. Ready to use in a week.

MRS. D. S. R.

PRESSED BEEF—SUPPER DISH.

Two pounds round beef steak chopped fine, one cup sweet milk, two tablespoons salt, one tablespoon black pepper, two soda crackers rolled fine, and one egg. Mix all well together with the hands, press into a bread-tin, and bake one hour and a half. When cold, cut in thin slices.

MRS. W. N. S.

BROILED STEAK, WITH MUSHROOMS.

One porter house steak, seasoned, and broiled rare. Take one-half cup butter and half a teaspoonful flour; let it brown in the pan, and pour in nearly a cup of boiling water, into which turn one small cupful of mushrooms; let them simmer ten minutes, then pour over the steak and serve.

MRS. BINGHAM.

MUTTON CHOPS WITH TOMATO SAUCE.

Take lean chops, salt, pepper, and dip in beaten eggs, then roll in cracker-crumbs, and fry in hot drippings. According to the number of chops, have tomatoes, canned or fresh, put through a sieve to strain out the seeds, and stewed till like a very thick cream. Season with salt, pepper and butter, pour on a hot platter, and then lay on the nicely browned chops.

MRS. D. S. R.

YORKSHIRE PUDDING, TO EAT WITH ROAST BEEF.

In a large bowl put a half pint flour, and half teaspoon of salt. Stir in *very* gradually one pint of milk, and four eggs beaten light,

USING PETTIT'S CIDER AND FRUIT PRESERVATIVE.

beating constantly and thoroughly. Pour into a greased pan, and bake from one-half to three-quarters of an hour. Serve immediately. MRS. C. T. V. S.

ENGLISH POT PIE.

Cut 1½ lbs. round steak into finger-lengths, and dust with flour. In an iron kettle, first heated, drop the fat, and then the lean meat, and after it has browned, one carrot, a turnip and an onion cut into small pieces. Stir briskly, and pour in one pint boiling water, seasoning to taste; let it come to a boil, then set where it will just simmer, covering closely. Make a crust of one cup chopped suet, two scant cups flour and a level teaspoon of salt. Toss together in a bowl, make a hole in the centre, pour in half a cup of cold water, and mix quickly with a knife, adding a few drops of water to bind the crumbs, but do not knead. Roll out a very little larger than the kettle, and an inch thick, and lay over the meat and vegetables, cover, and keep gently simmering for an hour. When ready to serve, cut the crust pie fashion, and lay on the platter around the meat. MRS. M. L. S.

HAMBURG STEAK.

Have a nice round steak (beef) chopped fine at the market. In a hot frying pan, put a tablespoon of butter; when melted, put in the meat, which has been seasoned with salt and pepper, and stir until the red look of the meat is changed, which will take about three minutes. MRS. HETTIE B. B.

STUFFING FOR ROAST FOWLS.

Take stale bread crumbs, rubbed fine, moisten slightly with milk; for a turkey, about two large tablespoonfuls of butter should be used, and mixed in a melted state; season with salt, pepper, a teaspoon of finely powdered summer savory, a little chopped celery, and an egg, if desired. Or small pieces of bread which have been dried in a cool oven, may be scalded with boiling water, *thoroughly* drained, and the butter and seasoning added. Plain mashed potatoes are sometimes used, with the same seasoning. For ducks and

---

TRY PRESERVING YOUR FRUIT WITHOUT HEAT,

geese, onion and sage should be used. For boiled fowl, oysters are often used; a pint to each turkey. The hearts, livers, gizzards of roast fowls should be boiled in salted water until tender, chopped very fine, and stirred with the water in which they have been cooked, into the dripping pan, after the fowl has been removed. Thicken with flour, to make the gravy. The fowls should be roasted slowly, and often basted, with the juices which escape from them into the pan.

CHICKENS.

Young chickens should be split open down the back, and broiled for 20 minutes over a clear fire, watching carefully that they do not burn. Put bits of butter over them, salt and pepper, and stand in the oven two minutes before serving. For fricassed chicken, cut up and put in a stew-kettle, with plenty of hot water; skim and salt, then cook slowly for one hour and a half or two hours, according to size and age, or until tender; then thicken the broth with a little flour, till about as thick as cream. It is more delicious to let the broth cook down pretty low, and add rich milk to make the gravy with. Another way of cooking chickens is to cut them open down the back as for broiling, steam for half an hour, and then finish them in a dripping-pan, in the oven, using the water over which they have been steamed, to put into the pan, for basting and gravy. Another nice way is to cut up the chicken as for a fricassee, cook in water (put on hot) till nearly done, then put into a dripping-pan with enough hot butter to brown nicely, turning each piece over, that both sides may brown. When done, take up and set in the oven for a few minutes; add to the butter remaining in pan, half a cup of hot water, then a pint of rich milk; thicken a little with flour, and put the chicken back into the gravy for about three minutes, when serve. A little chopped parsley may be added to gravy.

ESCALLOPED CHICKEN.

Cook two large chickens till very tender, seasoning with salt and pepper. Then cut into quite small pieces, and put a layer of it into a baking dish, alternately with layers of cracker crumbs and

USING PETTIT'S CIDER AND FRUIT PRESERVATIVE.

bits of butter. Repeat till dish is full, adding the broth in which chicken was cooked, to each layer, just enough to cover. Sprinkle crumbs over the top, put in oven and brown.

MRS. E. M'KINSTRY.

CHICKEN CROQUETTES.

Two cups chopped meat, one egg, one-half cup potatoes, mashed and seasoned well. Mix and make into rolls about three inches long, and fry in hot fat. MRS. M. L. S.

CHICKEN CROQUETTES, NO. 2.

To each pint minced fowl, add one-half pint cream, and season with pepper, salt, and a little finely minced parsley. Heat together in a stew-pan, and when boiling, thicken with one tablespoon each of butter and flour, first mixed to a smooth paste; cook a few minutes, then stir in the beaten yolks of two eggs, and remove from the fire. When cool roll into form, dip in egg, then in cracker crumbs, and fry.

In frying all croquettes, the fat (lard or dripping) must be very hot, and they are best done in a wire basket. The flavor may be varied by that of onion or lemon juice, and strong soup-stock may be used instead of cream, while finely powdered bread crumbs may take the place of flour. This recipe should make 18 croquettes.

MRS. M. L. S.

BROILED PARTRIDGE, WITH JELLY DRESSING.

Split bird down the back, broil and season with salt and pepper. For dressing, take butter the size of an egg, one-half cup currant jelly, heating first the butter thoroughly, then put in jelly and let simmer until the latter is entirely dissolved; pour over partridge and serve. MRS. BINGHAM.

TRY PRESERVING YOUR FRUIT WITHOUT HEAT,

SHELL FISH, ETC.

OYSTER SOUP.

Drain the liquor from one quart oysters, and add to it one quart of milk and water, mixed in any desired proportion; set on the stove and skim as it heats. When boiling, add salt and pepper to taste, and thicken with one tablespoon even full of flour, rubbed smooth with one large tablespoon of butter. Or, two tablespoons of very fine cracker crumbs may be used instead of flour. When ready to use, put in the oysters, and let them cook until the edges begin to curl, no longer. Serve at once. "E."

STEAMED OYSTERS.

Drain the liquor from the oysters, put it on the stove, let boil, skim, and season with butter, pepper and salt. Add the oysters, let them come to a boil, and serve at once. MRS. E. F. S.

OYSTER STEW.

Drain oysters, let liquor boil, and skim it; for one quart oysters, three-quarters pint of milk to the liquor; add salt, pepper and butter; when boiling, put in oysters, and cook just long enough to curl the edges. Have tureen hot, and serve.

FRIED OYSTERS.

Drain oysters thoroughly; roll all first in flour or very fine cracker dust; then take each in turn, dip in beaten egg, and again into the cracker dust. Let stand for half an hour, if possible, in a cool place, then fry quickly in very hot fat and serve immediately. "E."

OYSTER OMELETTE.

Whisk six eggs to a stiff froth, and add, by degrees, one cup of cream, or milk, and beat well together, seasoning with salt and pepper to taste. Have ready one dozen fine oysters cut in half; pour the egg and milk into a pan in which is a large tablespoon of

---

USING PETTIT'S CIDER AND FRUIT PRESERVATIVE.

melted butter, *hot;* drop the oysters evenly over the surface, fry a light brown, but do not turn. Serve at once. MRS. E. M'K.

OYSTER CAKES.

Chop very fine one-quarter pound veal, one quarter pound suet, and one pint solid oysters. Mix, add pepper and salt and enough cracker crumbs to make into small cakes. Dip into beaten egg and fry in butter. M. R.

DEVILED OYSTERS.

To one hundred oysters, chopped fine, add about half the quantity of bread crumbs, one-half cup butter, (melted.) one pint milk, salt, black and cayenne pepper; thicken with one tablespoon flour. Scrub large, deep oyster shells, and fill them with the mixture, sprinkling the tops with cracker dust, and bake till brown in hot oven. Patty-pans can be used instead of the shells.

MISS L. C. B.

CREAMED OYSTERS.

Take one quart large oysters, strain off the liquor, set it on the stove, boil and skim. In a kettle put one pint cream or milk, to which add one saltspoon salt, two tablespoons of rolled and sifted crackers, and one teaspoon of cornstarch, moistened with a little of the milk. Stir carefully until boiling, then add a teaspoon of butter, (if *milk* was used,) and boil up again, adding the oyster liquor. Meantime the drained oysters should have been placed in a colander or steamer, over boiling water, from five to eight minutes, or until edges shrivel. Put them in a hot dish, and pour cream over them. MRS. J. C. M'C.

OYSTER PIE.

Line a dish with puff paste; dredge well with flour; drain one quart of oysters, put into the dish, season with salt, pepper and butter; add some of the liquor, sprinkle rolled crackers over, then put on the top crust, leaving a small opening in the top for the steam to escape. Bake in a quick oven, served hot as possible.

MRS. FRASIER SPRAKER.

TRY PRESERVING YOUR FRUIT WITHOUT HEAT,

LITTLE PIGS IN BLANKETS.

Season large oysters with pepper, roll them in rolled crackers; cut bacon in thin slices, wrap an oyster in each slice, and fasten with a toothpick. Cook just long enough in a frying pan to cook the bacon—about two minutes. Serve on small pieces of toast, if desired. FLORENCE M. SPRAKER.

OYSTER PATTIES.

Make a puff paste of one pound flour, one pound butter, two eggs and a little water, one teaspoon baking powder. Roll out one-fourth of an inch thick, cut out a round piece for the bottom of patty, then cut in strips and wind around the edge until pyramid in shape; bake quickly.

CREAM OYSTER FOR FILLING PATTIES.

One quart of oysters, cooked in their liquor, and drained; in another kettle put one pint of milk, minced parsley, salt, one tablespoon flour rubbed smooth in milk; mix all these together, then boil, stirring carefully; add a generous lump of butter, (tablespoonful,) boil a while longer, put the oysters in a hot dish, pour the cream over them, and serve, or place carefully in the patty-shells. F. M. S.

PICKLED OYSTERS.

Scald oysters in salted water, which should be hot before putting them in. When they come to the top, skim them out, and lay them on a dry cloth. Strain the oyster liquor, boil and skim; put the oysters in a jar, and pour the hot liquor over them. To a gallon of oysters, use one quart of vinegar, one finely sliced lemon, and two tablespoons whole pepper. Heat the vinegar also; use count oysters. To keep in summer, put while hot in fruit jars and close tight. MRS. S. MORRELL.

CLAM SOUP.

To 20 or 25 clams chopped *fine*, add two quarts of boiling water, and when they boil up stir in one large tablespoonful of butter and two of flour, previously well rubbed together; let the whole simmer a few minutes, then stir in one pint milk and one egg, beaten together; take up immediately. MRS. M. F. SCHOLL.

STEWED CLAMS.

Let them stew slowly, with a little pepper, in their own liquor, for 15 or 20 minutes. Put slices of buttered toast in a dish, and pour over. *

CLAM CHOWDER.

Fry two slices salt pork in an iron pot; take it out in a few minutes, leaving the fat in the pot; put in a few thin slices of onion first. Have ready six potatoes cut into dice, one quart of clams chopped fine, six crackers rolled and the pork cut up small; put first a layer of potatoes, then of the clams, plenty of pepper and a little salt, and more onion; fill up the remainder in the same way, put in the liquor of the clams, and fill in with water enough to cover the chowder. Cook nearly half an hour, and just before taking-up, add one pint milk. This makes enough for eight people.
MRS. D. H. F.

LOBSTER BISQUE.

To one can lobster, four cups milk, three-fourths cup rolled crackers, four cups boiling water, two tablespoons butter, salt to taste, juice of a lemon, and cayenne pepper at discretion. Cut lobster small with knife, and put into the boiling water, with the salt and pepper, and cook 30 minutes. Heat the milk to boiling, and stir into it the cracker crumbs; when the lobster has cooked half an hour, stir in the butter, simmer five minutes, add the milk, stir well, and just before serving, put in lemon juice. Serve as a soup; and with it crackers and slices of lemon MRS. E. M'K.

LOBSTER SALAD.

Wash one head of lettuce, drain well, and shred in small pieces; cut or chop one lobster in small pieces, (canned lobster will do as well,) and mix lobster and lettuce together. Have ready the fol-

TRY PRESERVING YOUR FRUIT WITHOUT HEAT,

lowing dressing, and pour over the whole. Dressing.—Beat together the yolk of one hard boiled egg, (first rubbed smooth,) one raw egg, one teaspoon ground mustard, same of pepper, half-cup melted butter, half cup sugar, and the juice of one lemon, with one tablespoon of vinegar. MRS. M. L. S.

TIMBALE OF SALMON.

Remove bones, skin and oil from one can salmon, and mash through a sieve. Add gradually, beating all the time, four tablespoons of cream, and unbeaten whites of two eggs, until the whole is a smooth paste, and white; add salt and cayenne to taste. Fill mixture in small cups, and stand in a baking pan, half-filled with hot water. Bake 20 minutes; when done, turn out of cups, and pour drawn butter over.

CREAMED SALMON.

Turn one can of salmon into a colander, and drain, pick into small flakes with a fork, and remove all bits of bone and skin. Heat in a double boiler one cup of cream, and one-half cup milk, with a pinch of soda: rub together two even teaspoons of cornstarch and one tablespoon butter, salt and pepper, and stir into the boiling milk, not ceasing to stir until it has thickened and is smooth. Put in the salmon, and stir with a fork till hot. Fill scallop shells or patty pans, sprinkling cracker crumbs over, and small bits of butter. Bake a light brown. MRS. E. M'K.

SALMON CROQUETTES.

Drain and pick over one can salmon; mix with four soda crackers, rolled fine, the juice of one lemon, two well beaten eggs, butter the size of an egg, and season with salt and pepper. Make into balls, roll in cracker crumbs and the white of egg. Brown in hot lard.
MRS. D. S. MORRELL.

CODFISH BALLS.

Two cups fish, boiled and picked, four cups hot mashed potatoes, one and one-half tablespoons butter, three or four tablespoons of milk; mix and make into cakes, roll in crumbs, then in egg, then in crumbs again, and fry. MRS. C. T. V. S.

FISH BALLS NO. 2.

Equal parts of uncooked codfish, and potatoes fresh boiled and mashed, but not seasoned. Shred fish fine, wash twice in cold water, squeezing dry at last; add hot potatoes, and mix with spoon, till cool enough to use the hand. Season with pepper and a little salt, if necessary, add one egg, and butter the size of an egg, beating well. Dip hand into cold water, form mixture into small cakes, roll in flour or egg, and rolled cracker. Have hot lard or drippings in flat pan, one-quarter inch deep, and drop them in; when browned on one side, turn. Ten minutes will cook them. MRS. D. S. R.

FISH BALLS NO. 3.

One cup salt codfish, one pint of peeled and cut up potatoes, one egg, well beaten, one teaspoon butter, one-fourth salt spoon pepper. Wash the fish and pick into half inch pieces, and throw into cold water until ready. Put fish and potatoes in stew-pan, cover with boiling water and cook twenty-five minutes, or till potatoes are soft. Drain off water carefully, mash and beat the potatoes together until very light. Add butter and pepper, beat again till cool, and stir in beaten egg. Shape in a tablespoon, without smoothing, slip into a wire basket, and fry in boiling hot lard *one* minute. Drain on soft paper and send immediately to table. MRS. H. VAN E.

CREAMED CODFISH.

One quart codfish, shredded fine; wash in two or three waters, and squeeze dry. Put large tablespoon of butter in frying pan; when melted stir in fish, add large cup of milk or cream, let it boil up, set back from the fire, and stir in a well-beaten egg. Pour out on platter, and sprinkle over it two hard boiled eggs, chopped, and a little chopped parsley. MRS. C. T. VAN S.

TRY PRESERVING YOUR FRUIT WITHOUT HEAT,

POTTED FISH.

Take a fresh fish, herring, shad or other fish; clean, dry and cut in convenient size for packing in a stone jar; cover the bottom of the jar with slices of fish, sprinkle over salt, pepper, three or four allspice, the same of cloves, a bit of mace, and *small* bits of butter; then more layers, with spices as above, till the jar is nearly filled: cover with cider vinegar, but not too strong. Put tight cover on jar, and bake in slow oven for six hours. HETTIE B. B.

HALIBUT

May be cut in steaks, washed, and dried on cloth, rolled in flour, and fried in plenty of very hot lard or dripping. Or, a piece of from five to six pounds may be boiled for about an hour in water slightly salted, and in which is one tablespoon of vinegar. Serve with drawn butter, in which (for one-half pint) is stirred a hard-boiled egg, finely chopped.

SHAD

May be prepared for frying in same manner, taking care to have fat very hot; or it may be broiled and sent to table, seasoned lightly, and with bits of butter over it.

BLUE FISH

Is excellent fried or broiled, but is better to be baked, first being filled with this dressing: Bread crumbs, slightly moistened with milk, to which a tablespoon of butter has been added, season with salt, pepper, and a little chopped parsley or celery. When the fish is nearly done, having basted it several times with butter, turn a half cup of milk into the pan, which thicken at the last with flour and pour over the fish. E. F. S.

DEVILED CLAMS.

Take fifteen hard clams, have them opened raw, cut off the outside rim or hard part of the clam, chop the balance quite fine. Save a portion of the liquor to mix the clams with the bread dust or crumbs, of which take about three tablespoonfuls, or more if they seem very moist. Add three tablespoons melted butter, red pepper, and a very little Worcestershire sauce and salt, and mix soft. Have the clam shells thoroughly clean, and fill them with the mixture; sprinkle bread crumbs over them, and place them in oven until nicely browned. Serve hot, and garnish with parsley.

MRS. WILLIAM ARKELL.

OYSTER SALAD.

Take fifty small oysters, and cook in salted water until their edges begin to curl, then let them cool thoroughly. Cut about the same quantity, by measure, of celery in small pieces, put salt, pepper, vinegar, and a few drops of lemon juice with it; then add the oysters whole. Place on dish, and cover with mayonnaise dressing; garnish with sliced lemon, pickles, hard boiled eggs and parsley.

MRS. WM. A.

BOILED SARDINES ON TOAST.

Take fine large sardines, lifting carefully from box, and wipe off oil, or let it be absorbed by soft paper. Broil in fine toaster, and lay on narrow strips of buttered toast. Serve hot.

MRS. C. T. VAN S.

VEGETABLES.

STEWED POTATOES.

Bake six potatoes, and when cold, take off skin and chop fine. Put one pint of milk in a spider, with a tablespoon of butter, salt and pepper. When the milk boils, put in potatoes, heat thoroughly, turn in hot dish and serve.

MRS. C. G. PETTIT.

LYONAISE POTATOES.

One quart cold boiled potatoes cut in dice, three tablespoons butter, one of chopped onion. Fry onion in butter till it begins

---

TRY PRESERVING YOUR FRUIT WITHOUT HEAT,

to yellow: add potatoes, salt and pepper; stir with fork carefully. When well heated, add a little parsley, if desired, and cook two minutes longer. Serve on hot dish. CONTRIBUTED.

POTATOES ESCALLOPED.

Peel and slice six medium potatoes. Put in a baking dish a layer of potatoes, then one of bread crumbs, a little salt and small pieces of butter. Continue till all the potatoes are used, having bread crumbs on top. Cover with milk and bake forty-five minutes, or till potatoes are tender. Or boil potatoes first, not too well done. MRS. BINGHAM.

POTATO PUFF.

Two cups of mashed potatoes, two tablespoons melted butter, two well-beaten eggs, one cup milk.. Mix well and bake half an hour in quick oven. M. A. R.

POTATO BALLS OR CROQUETTES NO. 1.

Four large mealy potatoes, cold, mashed with two tablespoons melted butter, salt, pepper, tablespoon cream and beaten yolk of one egg. Rub together till very smooth. Shape into balls or small rolls; dip in beaten egg, then in sifted bread crumbs. Fry in boiling lard. MRS. ALICE GEORTNER.

POTATO CROQUETTES NO. 2.

One pint hot mashed potatoes, one tablespoon butter, half a saltspoon white pepper, half teaspoon of salt, yolk of one egg. Beat until very light. When cool add yolk and mix thoroughly. Rub through a sieve. Shape in balls, roll in bread crumbs, then in beaten egg, again in crumbs. Fry in hot lard one minute. Drain and serve. MRS. ANNIE TAYLOR.

POTATO SOUFFLE.

Bake six potatoes. When done, cut off just the top. Scrape the inside out, being careful of shells. Mash and season with but-

---

USING PETTIT'S CIDER AND FRUIT PRESERVATIVE.

ter, salt and cream. Whites of two eggs, beaten stiff, mix in lightly. Fill the shells with mixture, set on a tin, and bake ten or fifteen minutes. MRS. ALICE WATSON.

POTATO SALAD.

One quart boiled potatoes, sliced; one teacup cabbage, shredded; one small onion, tablespoon and a half of butter, the same quantity of drippings. Fry onion in dripping, with one tablespoon of flour, till it begins to yellow. Add a half cup vinegar. Stir in potatoes and cabbage, and pour over two tablespoons sweet cream. Season to taste with salt and pepper. MRS. M. L. S.

SLICED CUCUMBERS.

Cut in thin slices, throw into salted water, and put in a cool place for an hour. When ready to serve, drain the water off, season with salt, pepper and a very little vinegar, stirring in at last (for a pint) one-half cup of thick sour cream. Eat with cayenne pepper.

BAKED TOMATOES.

Peel them, and put in bottom of baking dish, cutting in half if they are large, and putting the cut side up. Sprinkle over with a thin layer of bread crumbs, salt, pepper and small bits of butter, and repeat until dish is full, having crumbs on top. Bake one hour in a brisk oven. " E."

ESCALLOPED TOMATOES.

Take stewed tomatoes, canned or fresh, put in baking dish in alternate layers with bread crumbs, salt, pepper and bits of butter. Bake half an hour. " E."

BOSTON BAKED BEANS.

Put one pint white beans (pea beans are considered best) in cold water at night. In the morning drain off, put on hot water more than to cover, small piece of salt pork two and a half or three inches square. Season with salt—not too much, as the pork will

TRY PRESERVING YOUR FRUIT WITHOUT HEAT,

add some—pepper, tablespoon molasses. Pour in earthen jar or bean pot, set pork in the top, cover and bake in slow oven all day. Look in occasionally, and if too dry add hot water. When done should be very moist but not watery. MRS. HETTIE B. BULLOCK.

CREAM TURNIPS.

Peel, slice, and cut in inch-square pieces, and stew the turnips till tender. Make a sauce of a cup of milk. Put in a double boiler, and when hot stir in a tablespoon of butter that has been mixed with half a spoon corn starch or flour ; season with pepper and salt. Drain the turnips, turn into the boiler and let stand for ten minutes. Do not let it boil. MRS. E. M'K.

PARSNIP CAKES.

Boil soft and mash smooth six medium-size parsnips. Season with salt, pepper and butter. Add one egg, beaten light. Drop from spoon into a pan in which is some butter, hot. Fry brown on both sides. MRS. M'C.

FRIED TOMATOES.

Select medium sized smooth tomatoes, not too ripe. Cut in slices one inch thick. Sprinkle a little salt and pepper over them, dip in beaten egg, then in rolled crackers or bread crumbs. Fry in a little hot lard, carefully turning when brown on one side, and serve with following sauce : mix one tablespoon flour smoothly with one pint milk, using very little till perfectly smooth, add tablespoon butter creamed, beat all into the milk, with one well-beaten egg, a little salt and pepper, and a little mace, if liked. Place stew-pan on range and let simmer till it thickens. Put tomatoes on a hot dish, pour sauce around, and serve ; or, after tomatoes have been taken from pan, put in a half cup boiling water, thicken with a little browned flour, boil up and pour over tomatoes. Green tomatoes prepare in the same way, omitting cream sauce.

MRS. M. SMITH.

USING PETTIT'S CIDER AND FRUIT PRESERVATIVE.

TOMATOES WITH MAYONNAISE.

Smooth medium tomatoes, carefully skinned, the stem end cut out and piled with a mayonnaise, makes a very pretty as well as good dish.   CONTRIBUTED.

CORN OYSTERS.

Grate eight ears of sweet corn, or cutting down through the centre of kernels, scrap out, add two eggs, two tablespoons flour, a little salt. Stir together and dip with large spoon into frying pan with hot lard, in cakes; turn when brown.   MRS. M'C.

CORN PUDDING.

Three well beaten eggs, one quart milk, one quart corn cut and scraped from the ear, or canned corn chopped fine. Salt and pepper to taste. two teaspoons butter. Bake half an hour. If corn is fresh use two quarts of milk and bake an hour and a half.

CONTRIBUTED.

MACARONI.

Break and wash 12 sticks macaroni, put in two quarts boiling waetr with one tablespoon salt, boil 25 minutes, pour off water. Prepare one-half cup grated cheese, one-half cup of bread crumbs. Put a layer of macaroni in a baking dish, sprinkle over some cheese and bread crumbs, a little pepper, salt, and some bits of butter. Repeat till all is used; poke a hole in the centre. Pour over all one-half pint cream sauce, sprinkle crumbs and cheese on top, set in oven to brown about one-half hour.

CREAM SAUCE FOR MACARONI.

One pint cream or milk, one big tablespoon flour. Let half of cream come to boil; flour mixed smooth in the remainder; stir in the boiling cream and boil three minutes. Use half for the amount of macaroni mentioned.   MRS. N. S. B.

MACARONI PLAIN.

Wash and break in pieces, six sticks of macaroni, or eight of spaghetti; put in salted water and boil until tender but not broken, about

---

TRY PRESERVING YOUR FRUIT WITHOUT HEAT,

20 minutes. Drain and put a layer in a baking dish; over this some grated cheese and pieces of butter. Then more macaroni, cheese and butter, a little salt. Put over all milk or cream, till you can see it, or bread crumbs can be added. Bake one-half hour, or till a nice brown. R.

SALADS AND DRESSINGS.

SALAD DRESSING No. 1.

Six eggs beaten light, half teacup melted butter, one coffee cup cream, one tablespoon mustard rubbed with tablespoon of sugar, one coffee cup good vinegar. Cook until of the consistency of custard, over hot water. For two chickens the above quantity is sufficient; take one-third chicken, two-thirds celery, pick the meat when hot; chop celery; pepper and salt to taste.
MRS. S. A. R.

CABBAGE SALAD.

Shred cabbage fine, salt and pepper, one cup of vinegar, one large tablespoon of melted butter, one tablespoon sugar. Put in sauce pan and boil, pour hot on cabbage and cover. Stir in lightly with a fork, two tablespoons sour cream just before serving. Prepared in the morning.
MRS. S. A. R.

CELERY SALAD.

Cut the celery into pieces about a half an inch long; pour over salad dressing No. 1.
MRS. S. A. R.

MAYONNAISE DRESSING.

One hour before using, place on ice a soup plate, silver fork, two eggs, and a bottle of table oil. Prepare in a cool room. Take the cold plate, break yolks of eggs on it and begin to stir, *only one way*—then oil, a drop at a time, constantly stirring till you have used one-fourth of a large sized bottle. Add half a teaspoon mixed

USING PETTIT'S CIDER AND FRUIT PRESERVATIVE.

mustard, a very little red pepper and salt to taste, the juice of half a lemon, constantly stirring till all the ingredients are in. Vinegar may be used inplace of lemon, and more added if too rich. Set on ice until wanted. MRS. C. T. VAN S.

FRENCH DRESSING.

Two tablespoons of oil to one of vinegar; pepper and salt to taste. For water cresses, garnish dish with cold boiled eggs, and pour over the dressing or serve in sauce tureen; also use for lettuce, and lettuce and tomatoes together. MRS. C. T. VAN S.

PREPARED MUSTARD.

Two eggs, two small teaspoons salt, three tablespoons mustard two small cups of vinegar, one tablespoon of sugar, a *small* pinch of cayenne pepper. Cook until it thickens.

MAYONNAISE DRESSING.

Yolk of one egg, half teaspoon dry mustard; mix well, then drop in oil, stirring constantly until it is very thick; thin with vinegar; if more dressing is required, add slowly more oil, and then vinegar, then half teaspoon salt, the juice of half a lemon. Stir with silver fork. MRS. J. C. M'C.

TRY PRESERVING YOUR FRUIT WITHOUT HEAT,

EGGS.

PICKLED EGGS.

Boil the eggs hard; when cold remove the shells. Lay them carefully in a jar, pour over them scalded vinegar, well flavored with whole cloves, allspice to suit the taste; also pepper and salt. When cold close the jar closely. MRS. F. S.

DEVILED EGGS.

Boil six eggs hard; when cold remove the shells and cut in two with a sharp knife. Cut the yolks in a bowl, rub smooth, add teaspoon soft butter, a pinch of salt, a sprinkle of pepper, a little vinegar. Fill the white portion of the eggs with this mixture; put parsley or lettuce on a plate and arrange the eggs on it.

ANNA M'C. PETTIT.

POACHED EGGS.

Have the water hot and salted. Break each egg separately in a saucer, slip carefully from saucer to the water; boil slowly; when done remove with a skimmer; trim neatly. Put each egg on a square piece of buttered toast, or on a thin slice of broiled ham.

MRS. F. SPRAKER.

BAKED EGGS, No. 1.

Butter a smooth tin, break the eggs in a saucer one by one, and slip into the pan; do not crowd so as to break the yolks. Put a bit of butter and a sprinkle of salt on each egg. Set them into the oven, bake until the whites are set; if the oven is right it will take but a few minutes. CONTRIBUTED.

BAKED EGGS, No. 2.

Take as many eggs as needed—separate carefully so as not to break the yolks. Beat the whites to a stiff froth: spread the whites on the tin, then carefully drop the yolks in the froth one by one; sprinkle with salt, set in a hot oven and bake five minutes.

CONTRIBUTED.

USING PETTIT'S CIDER AND FRUIT PRESERVATIVE.

OMELET.

Four eggs, one cup of milk, one tablespoon of flour, a little salt. Beat the whites of the eggs to a froth; add last. Put a little butter in the spider, cover closely, cook in a few minutes. xxx.

BOILED EGGS.

Put into a kettle of boiling water with a spoon; be careful not to crack the shell; if desired soft, let them boil two and a half or three minutes; if hard, six minutes.

BAKED EGGS, No. 3.

Take one dozen hard boiled eggs, cut in halves, remove the yolks, whip them lightly with finely chopped boiled ham, well seasoned; put this mixture back into the whites, make a sauce of drawn butter, put the eggs in a pudding dish, pour the sauce over them; sprinkle a few bread crumbs and a little chopped ham over this; bake until slightly brown. Serve hot.

MRS. CLARA T. VAN STEENBURGH.

PLAIN OMELET.

Separate six eggs, beat the whites to a stiff froth, the yolks very smooth; to each yolk add a teaspoon of milk, beat well, lastly stir in the whites lightly. Have ready a hot frying pan with a lump of butter; pour in the mixture. Do not stir, but as soon as it begins to set, slip a knife under around the edge, letting the mixture through. While a little soft on top, set into a hot oven a few minutes; place a hot dish bottom upwards on the top of the pan, and upset or roll it on the dish. MRS. D. S. R.

TO TELL GOOD EGGS.

Put them in cold water; if they sink, or the large end turns up, they are not fresh.

TRY PRESERVING YOUR FRUIT WITHOUT HEAT,

BREAKFAST AND SUPPER CAKES AND DISHES.

HOP YEAST.

Take one large handful of hops, put in bag and place in pot with four quarts cold water; let it boil hard for 20 minutes. Then pour slowly over one quart unsifted flour, stirring fast while pouring. When milk warm, add tablespoon salt, one of ginger, two of molasses, and a cup of yeast or two yeast cakes. Let stand 24 hours, stirring often, then put in a jug; do not press the cork tight. Keep in cool place. MRS. W. N. SCHOLL.

FRENCH ROLLS.

Two quarts flour, piece of butter size of an egg, two eggs, salt spoon of salt. Rub butter and flour together, beat eggs well and add with salt three-fourths of a cup yeast, and milk enough to make a soft dough. (If in cold weather milk should be warm.) Knead and set to rise. When light, knead again lightly, roll out and cut in cakes one-fourth inch thick. Put in warm place to rise, and bake in quick oven. Can be mixed at night for breakfast, or in the morning for supper. MRS E. F. S.

ROLLS OR TEA BISCUIT.

Scald one pint of milk, add one tablespoon sugar, little salt, butter half the size of an egg, one egg. When lukewarm, stir in three-fourths cup of yeast, or small yeast cake; flour to make a stiff batter; let rise and knead as often as it gets light. Roll and cut out one hour before baking. MRS. S. A. R.

BROWN BREAD, No. 1.

One pint of corn meal, two of rye flour, half cup molasses, small tablespoon soda. Mix with warm water, thin enough to pour into a greased pail. Or it may be mixed with buttermilk or sour milk, using a little more soda. Steam three or four hours until it begins to shrink from the pail. MRS. H. D. WALKER.

USING PETTIT'S CIDER AND FRUIT PRESERVATIVE.

GRAHAM BREAD.

One quart of warm water, a little salt, a heaped quart of graham flour, three-fourths of a cup of yeast, one cup of molasses. Stir together and set to rise over night. In the morning mix with wheat flour, stiff enough to form into loaves; let rise, then bake one hour and a quarter.

BROWN BREAD, No. 2.

Two cups sweet milk, one of sour milk, two of corn meal, one of wheat flour, one-half cup molasses, teaspoon soda. Scald sweet milk, pour on corn meal, stirring; when cold add other ingredients. Steam three hours, then put in hot oven to dry. MRS. N. S. B.

CORN BREAD.

Two and one-half cups flour, one large cup of meal, two teaspoons cream tartar, one of soda, three eggs, one cup of sugar, one pint of milk, two tablespoons melted butter. Mix well together and bake in hot oven. MRS. J. H. NELLIS.

FOX'S CORN MUFFINS.

One cup of flour, one-half cup meal, one-half teaspoon of salt, two and one-half baking powder, heaped tablespoon of butter. Beat well, and bake in a hot oven.

CORN CAKE.

One cup of flour, two-thirds of a cup of meal, one-third cup of sugar, one egg, one tablespoon melted butter, one cup of milk, three teaspoons baking powder, a little salt. Bake in quick oven 30 minutes.

PARKER HOUSE ROLLS.

One pint milk scalded, one tablespoon butter melted in milk, one of sugar, a teaspoon of salt, one-half cup of yeast, or one-fourth of a cake of compressed yeast dissolved in a half cup of warm water, six or seven cups of flour. When the milk is cool enough, add yeast, then the flour gradually, that it may not be too stiff. When light, stir down and let rise again. Roll, and cut out: put in pans, let rise till ready for the oven. MRS. H. D. W.

TRY PRESERVING YOUR FRUIT WITHOUT HEAT,

PARKER HOUSE ROLLS No. 2.

Into one pint boiling milk, put one-half cup butter. When cool, add one-fourth cup white sugar, one-half cup yeast, and a pinch of salt. Have two quarts sifted flour, make a hole in centre, and pour in mixture. Do this at night, next morning mix and knead well. Roll out in afternoon, cutting half inch thick; rub a little butter on top, and fold over. When light, wash top with sweet milk, and bake twenty minutes in quick oven. E. F. S.

BREAKFAST ROLLS.

Take a piece of bread dough after it has been mixed and raised in the morning. Roll a half inch thick, cut with a knife, one inch wide and four inches long; have ready a kettle of hot lard, drop them in and fry like cruller. Serve hot. MRS. M. F. S.

SODA BISCUIT.

One quart of flour, four teaspoons baking powder, piece of butter size of egg. Mix baking powder thoroughly in flour, then the butter. Use sweet milk enough to make as soft as you can roll. Bake in quick oven. Will made 30 biscuit. C. T. VAN S.

DROP BISCUIT.

One pint of flour, one dessertspoon butter rubbed in the flour until like sand; one small spoon salt, two teaspoons sugar, one small teaspoon baking powder. Rub all thoroughly together. Take a scant half pint of milk, make a hole in middle of flour and pour in; make a stiff batter, drop on pan and bake in hot oven.

MRS. M. L. S.

GRAHAM GEMS, No. 1.

One pint milk, one cup graham flour, one cup wheat flour, one egg, a pinch of salt. Bake in hot oven.

GRAHAM GEMS, No. 2.

One well beaten egg, pinch of salt, one pt. of sour milk and cream, one teaspoon soda. Graham flour to make a stiff batter. Bake in quick oven. MRS. W. N. S.

USING PETTIT'S CIDER AND FRUIT PRESERVATIVE.

OAT MEAL.

For eight persons take one cup prepared oat meal, two cups luke warm water, ½ teaspoon salt. Boil fifteen minutes in double boiler.

CEREALINE MUFFINS.

Two cups cerealine, two cups wheat flour, into which has been sifted two teaspoons baking powder, one teaspoon salt; then add two well beaten eggs, milk sufficient to make a soft batter. Bake in gem pans in a quick oven. MRS. W. N. S.

FLANNEL CAKES.

One quart of milk, one tablespoon butter melted in the milk, put aside till cool. Beat well five eggs, stir into milk with three pints of sifted flour, small teaspoon salt, one and a half tablespoons yeast. Should be light in three or four hours if kept near the fire. Bake on a griddle.

WHEAT CAKES.

One pt. thick sour milk, one pt. of flour, mixed together at night. In the morning add one well beaten egg, one teaspoon soda, pinch of salt. Bake on griddle. MRS. MCC.

SYRUP FOR CAKES.

Ten lbs. sugar and two qts. of water will make one gal. syrup. Put sugar and water in a pan or preserving kettle. Set on back of range; stir occasionally till dissolved, then let it heat till clear, but do not let it get boiling hot. R.

POP OVERS, No. 1.

One and a half cups flour, one and a half cups milk, three eggs, pinch of salt, tablespoon sugar. Put in gem pan, start in slow oven, hot oven towards the last. MRS. C. T. VAN S.

TRY PRESERVING YOUR FRUIT WITHOUT HEAT,

POP OVERS, No. 2.

Two cups flour, two eggs, one pt. milk, one heaped teaspoon baking powder, little salt. Beat twenty minutes, put in gem pans, or cups. Bake twenty minutes in hot oven. HETTIE B. B.

RAISED WAFFLES.

One qt. of flour, one pt. sweet milk, lukewarm, two eggs, two tablespoons melted butter, teaspoon salt, half teacup of yeast.
MRS. D. SPRAKER.

DEUTSCHE KUCHEN.

Make a sponge of one pint of warm sweet milk, one half yeast cake at night; set to rise. In the morning add a cup of milk, half a cup of butter, two tablespoons of sugar, a pinch of cinnamon, and salt; flour enough to knead soft. Let rise again; when light, roll in sheets one half inch thick, let rise again, then spread melted butter over the top; sprinkle with sugar and cinnamon. Will make two cakes in round tins. Or take a pint of light bread sponge, and add milk, &c. MRS. B. C. FOX.

WHEAT MUFFINS.

One pint flour, one tablespoon butter rubbed in flour, one egg, three small teaspoons baking powder, sweet milk to make batter like wheat cakes. Bake in hot oven in muffin tins.
MISS OLLIE WAGNER.

BLUEBERRY CAKE.

One-half cup sugar, one egg, one small cup milk, one and a half cups flour, large tablespoon butter, large teaspoon baking powder, cup berries, pinch of salt. Bake in quick oven fifteen minutes.
MRS. H. WALKER.

SALLY LUNN.

One scant pint flour, two eggs, one teacup milk, one-half teacup of butter, two heaped teaspoons baking powder. Beat eggs separately, adding whites last. Bake in pan or loaf about half an hour

S. A. R.

PUFFS.

One cup buttermilk, one egg, half teaspoon soda, a little salt. Mix very soft, roll thin, cut in small strips or squares, and drop in hot lard. To be eaten with maple syrup. MRS. S. A. R.

GEMS.

One egg, one cup of milk, one of flour, or enough to make a batter a little thicker than pancakes. Pinch of salt, two teaspoons baking powder. Heat gem pans hot, butter them, then pour in batter. Bake in quick oven twenty minutes. CONTRIBUTED.

MUFFINS.

Melt a piece of butter half the size of an egg, in one pint of milk. Stir in one egg, a half cup of yeast, or half a yeast cake, one lb. of flour. Set to rise over night. Bake on griddle in muffin rings, adding a half teaspoon soda dissolved in hot water.

CONTRIBUTED.

HOMINY FRITTERS.

One cup cooked hominy, one pint milk, two eggs, a little salt, two teaspoons baking powder, flour to make a stiff batter. Drop in hot lard. MRS. S. A. R.

CHEESE CANAPIES.

Cut slices of bread half an inch thick, then with a large round cutter, cut circles, these cut in half—they are not the true crescent shape that canopies should be, but will answer. Put a tablespoon of butter in a small sauce-pan (because to fry so little the butter required would be twice as much if you used a frying-pan,) and fry to a light brown. When done take them up and grate cheese over them, adding pepper and salt. Put them on a tin, to be set in the oven, until the meat goes on to the table. MRS. M. L. S.

TRY PRESERVING YOUR FRUIT WITHOUT HEAT,

FRITTERS.

One pound and a quarter of flour, four eggs, one pint and a half of milk. Beat yolks light, add to the milk and stir into the flour. Beat whites stiff, stir in, adding a pinch of salt, and a heaped teaspoon baking powder. Drop by the tablespoonful into hot lard and fry like crullers. MRS. E. F. S.

APPLE FRITTERS,

Are made by taking apples pared and cored, without dividing. Cut them in thin round slices and put one in each spoonful of batter. MRS. E. F. S.

RICE CROQUETTES.

One cup of rice boiled with water and salt, one-half cup of sugar, one quart of milk. Boil until thick, then stir in two eggs, roll in sifted bread crumbs. Sauce: one-half glass currant jelly, one small glass sherry wine, boil until a little thick. Pour it over the croquettes, and serve at once. CLARA T. VAN STEENBERGH.

JELLY SAUCE FOR RICE CROQUETTES.

One half cup boiling water, half cup currant jelly, two teaspoons corn starch, one tablespoon soft butter; wet the corn starch with a little water, then stir it in the boiling water; cook until it thickens, then add the butter; last, beat the jelly in and pour it over the croquettes. MRS. E. M'KINSTRY.

CHEESE STRAWS.

Mix two tablespoons of butter, four tablespoons of flour, four tablespoons of grated cheese, one egg, half teaspoon salt, a pinch of cayenne pepper. When these ingredients are well mixed together, roll out as thin as possible. Cut in strips one-quarter inch wide and three inches long. Bake them a nice brown. MRS. M. L. S.

FRIED CREAM.

One pint of milk, a full half teacup of sugar, butter the size of a hickory nut, yolks of three eggs, two tablespoons of corn starch, one tablespoon flour, a generous half cup full, all together; half teaspoon of vanilla, a stick of cinnamon one inch long; put cinnamon in the milk when it is about to boil, then stir in the sugar, corn starch and flour, two latter mixed together and rubbed smooth with two or three tablespoons of (extra) cold milk; stir it over the fire for fully two minutes, to cook the starch and flour. After taking it from the fire stir in the well beaten yolks of the eggs, return to the fire to set them, then remove from the fire: take out cinnamon stick, stir in butter and vanilla; pour it out on a buttered tin two-thirds of an inch thick. When cold and stiff cut into parallelograms, about two inches long by two wide; roll them carefully, first in sifted cracker crumbs, then in slightly sweetened and beaten egg, then again in the cracker crumbs; put in a wire basket, dip in hot lard until fried a light brown color; put in a hot oven four or five minutes, to better soften the pudding. Sprinkle over with pulverized sugar and serve. MRS. M. L. SMITH.

PIES.

PIE CRUST.

The easiest receipt for pie crust is the following. Three large cups flour, one cup lard, three-fourths cup water, half a salt spoon salt. This will make two round pies. Always use the best lard, and have it cold; put it into the flour and salt, and with a knife cut it into tiny pieces. Pour in the water gradually, stirring constantly with knife, and do not touch with the hands until you have got it all together, and handle as little as possible, in rolling out. In summer take ice water. It will need a little more water in winter than in summer.

This crust may be varied by taking part butter instead of all lard, and can be made with *more* shortening, if desired. To flake it for the upper crust, roll out lightly in a long strip, upon which place very small bits of butter, and a little sprinkling of flour. Roll like rolled sponge cake, cut across, and turn on end to roll out, sprinkling lightly with flour. Use always fresh dough for top crust.

TRY PRESERVING YOUR FRUIT WITHOUT HEAT,

PENNSYLVANIA APPLE PIE.

Line a pie plate with crust, then fill the dish full of apples, peeled, halved and cored. Mix together and pour over them, one cup sugar, half-cup cold water and one tablespoon flour, adding a few very small bits of butter. Bake till apples are cooked; have ready the whites of two eggs, beaten to a stiff froth, with two tablespoons pulverized sugar. Pour over top of pie and smooth, and return to oven a few minutes to brown slightly. Eat warm.

MRS. A. M'C. P.

APPLE PIE.

One-half pound of apples, boiled and well mashed, $\frac{1}{4}$ pound of butter beaten to a cream, mixed with the apples before they are cold, three eggs well beaten, $\frac{1}{2}$ pound sugar, one lemon juice and grated rind. Bake in a puff paste—no upper crust.

MRS. J. C. M'C.

APPLE MERINGUE PIE.

Stew some good pie apples and sweeten. Beat smooth and season with nutmeg. Line your dish with a good crust, fill with apples and bake. Make a meringue with the whites of three eggs, using two tablespoons of powdered sugar to each egg. If desired, flavor with rose water or vanilla. Beat till it will stand alone, and spread over the pie. Set back in the oven till colored a delicate brown. Eat cold. Very fine made with peaches.

MRS. S. A. R.

PUMPKIN PIE.

To one coffee cup stewed pumpkin pressed through a sieve, take one or two eggs, one pint new milk, sugar to make quite sweet, one-quarter teaspoon ginger, one-half cinnamon, or use nutmeg instead. Bake one hour in good crust. Squash pie is made precisely like pumpkin, only a little less of the squash. To make the pumpkin a darker colored pie, add more spice and a tablespoon of molasses.

MRS. D. S. R.

USING PETTIT'S CIDER AND FRUIT PRESERVATIVE.

LEMON PIE.

For one pie, two lemons; juice and grated rind, two cups of sugar, one cup of milk, two tablespoons of corn starch, the yolks of four eggs. Cook together the corn strach and milk, add the other ingredients, and bake in a puff paste. Beat the whites of the eggs with six tablespoons of powdered sugar and pour over the custard ; put pie in oven, and brown slightly. MRS. J. C. M'C.

LEMON PIE, No. 2.

Grate rind and strain juice of two lemons. Pare, core and chop fine one large tart apple. Pound one soft cracker fine. Melt two teaspoons butter and mix with cracker crumbs. Mix lemon rind and juice with apple, and stir in two cups sugar. Beat yolks of two eggs to thick froth, then whites to stiffness, then both together. Beat these with lemon, apple and sugar. Mix buttered crumbs with all, and bake till crust is done.

LEMON TARTS.

The grated rind and juice of one lemon ; add to this one cup of sugar, the yolk of one egg, and a large cup of cold water, into which has been stirred a dessert spoonful of cornstarch. Then cook until it is a clear straw colored jelly. Fill the paste shells, (which have been baked) with the jelly. Make a meringue with the white of the egg and two dessert spoonsful of powdered sugar. Cover the jelly with the meringue and stand in oven until a delicate brown. This will fill one dozen tarts. MRS. W. N. SCHOLL.

LEMON PRESERVE FOR TARTS.

One lb. sugar, one-quarter lb. butter, six eggs, leaving out the whites of two ; juice and grated rind of two lemons. Cook slowly until the consistency of honey, stirring all the time.

MRS. J. C. M'C.

TRY PRESERVING YOUR FRUIT WITHOUT HEAT,

FILLING FOR LEMON PIE.

Put one and one-half cups boiling water in a sauce pan on the stove, then stir thick with two tablespoons cornstarch, one cup sugar, (powdered) the yolks of three eggs, juice of two lemons or three if necessary, a little salt, a little butter. Pour into crust and bake. Beat whites of eggs, add one teaspoonful of sugar, put on pie when baked, and brown over.   CLARA VAN STEENBERG.

PEACH PIE.

Peel and halve peaches; line a pie plate with crust, lay in the fruit, sprinkle liberally over them sugar and a little water. Bake with an upper crust or with cross bars of paste over the top.

MRS. FRASIER SPRAKER.

PINE APPLE PIE.

One pineapple chopped fine, one-half cup water, two eggs, two cups sugar, three tablespoonfuls flour. To be made with two crusts and will be enough for two pies.   FLORENCE M. SPRAKER.

PINE APPLE PIE.

One teacup grated pineapple, one-half teacup water, one-half teacup sugar, yolks of two eggs, two even tablespoons cornstarch. Put in a pie dish lined with crust and bake half an hour.

ORANGE PIE.

Grate the rind from two large oranges, squeeze out the juice, beat four eggs and stir into them a cup of powdered sugar, add one-half teacup melted butter, after which add the orange with half pint milk or cream. Bake in a puff paste like a custard.

MRS. J. C. M'C.

BANANA PIE.

Line a pie plate with rich crust and bake. Slice three or four bananas fine, according to size, and fill the crust when cold; sprinkle a little sugar over them. Whip a teacup of sweetened cream very light and spread over the pie.   MRS. ALICE WATSON.

USING PETTIT'S CIDER AND FRUIT PRESERVATIVE.

MINCE MEAT.

Boil four or five lbs. beef (solid meat) till tender. Chop fine, and to each bowlful of chopped meat, take two of chopped apples; add one lb. chopped suet, two lbs. seeded raisins, (chopped) one lb. currants, half lb. figs, also chopped, two lbs. sugar, half pt. molasses, salt, a *little* pepper, cloves, cinnamon and mace (ground) to taste. Moisten well with cider, adding boiled cider, if you can procure it; and after mixing, put in large pan and cook for half an hour, when more spices and cider can be added, if needed. This may be canned like fruit, and set away for months. MRS. A. M'C. P.

CREAM PIE, No. 1.

Make an under crust for the pie and bake; when done, fill with the following: three cups of milk, three tablespoons cornstarch, three eggs(the yolks only,)one cup sugar,a little salt. Cook until it thickens. Beat the whites of the eggs to a stiff froth, with a little sugar, and brown. FLORENCE M. SPRAKER.

CREAM PIE, No. 2.

With the yolks of two eggs, mix one-half cup sugar, one large tablespoon flour, a little salt, one pint cold milk, let thicken on the range. Flavor to suit taste. Put in a baked crust and bake eight minutes. Frosting made with the whites of the eggs and sugar; a tablespoon of jelly added makes it very nice.

MRS. M. L. SMITH.

CHOCOLATE PIE.

Two cups of milk, yolks of two eggs, two-thirds cup sugar, two tablespoons cornstarch, two tablespoons grated chocolate. Heat the milk, sugar and chocolate together, add the cornstarch mixed in a little cold milk, then add the beaten yolks. Let all come to a boil. Line a pie tin with good pie crust, bake, then pour in the chocolate cream. Make a meringue of the two whites of eggs.

MRS. E. MC KINSTRY.

TRY PRESERVING YOUR FRUIT WITHOUT HEAT,

STRAWBERRY SHORT CAKE.

Take one quart of flour, sift into it two teaspoons of baking powder, a little salt, three tablespoons of butter well rubbed through ; add sweet milk enough to make soft dough, divide into two parts, roll each flat the same size, put one on top of the other and bake; when done they will separate. Spread on plenty of butter. Have the strawberries washed and drained, slightly crushed ; spread them on the crust, sprinkle well with sugar, put on the upper crust also well spread with butter.

MRS. FRASIER SPRAKER.

SAUCE FOR STRAWBERRY SHORT CAKE.

Take one-half cup butter, one and one-half cups sugar beaten to a cream, one pint strawberries mashed ; mix together, add whites of two eggs beaten light. MRS. D. H. F.

USING PETTIT'S CIDER AND FRUIT PRESERVATIVE.

PUDDINGS.

VELVET PUDDING.

Five eggs, beaten separately. One teacup of white sugar. Four tablespoons corn starch, dissolved in a little cold milk, added to yolks and sugar. Boil three pints sweet milk, and pour into it the yolks and sugar while boiling. Remove from fire when it becomes quite thick. Flavor with vanilla and pour into a baking dish. Beat the whites to a stiff froth with one-half cup white sugar, then pour over the top of pudding, and return to oven until slightly brown. To be eaten with sauce.   MRS. ALICE C. GEORTNER.

ORANGE PUDDING.

One quart of milk, three eggs, two dessert-spoons corn-starch. Use yolks, corn-starch and milk, and make a boiled custard. Let it stand until cold. Peel and slice four oranges, with two cups sugar. Pour custard over oranges and stir all together. Then beat whites and add a little sugar, and pour over, whole. Set in the oven to brown. Let it get very cold before serving.

MRS. ALICE C. GEORTNER.

PRUNE PUDDING.

One half pound prunes, stewed soft, and stones taken out. Let cool before using. Whites of five eggs, beaten stiff. Then beat the prunes in the eggs, a little at a time. Stir in three tablespoons of sugar. Bake in a buttered dish until a nice brown. Bake in moderate oven. Eaten with whipped cream.

MRS. N. S. BRUMLEY.

FLORENTINE PUDDING.

Make a sponge cake of six eggs, and bake in four cakes, in jelly tins. Beat the yolks of four eggs with four tablespoons of sugar. Pour one quart boiling milk on beaten eggs, stirring rapidly all the time. Then return to fire. Make a paste with three tablespoons corn starch mixed with a little cold milk, which stir at

---

TRY PRESERVING YOUR FRUIT WITHOUT HEAT.

once into custard on fire. Boil until thickened, stirring all the time. Flavor while hot with one teaspoon vanilla. Put one layer of this, when cold, between two of the cakes. Make chocolate icing of three tablespoons grated chocolate, six tablespoons sugar, two of cream, a small piece butter. Let it simmer a few minutes. While hot spread over top of pudding and sprinkle with sugar.

MISS LIDIE BAUM.

SPONGE PUDDING.

One-quarter cup of sugar, one-quarter cup of butter, one-half cup flour, five eggs, one pint boiled milk. Mix sugar and flour with a little cold milk and stir into boiling milk. Cook until it thickens and is smooth. Add butter, then well-beaten yolks of eggs. Lastly, whites beaten stiff. Bake in shallow dish, placed in pan of hot water, in hot oven. To be eaten with "Sea Foam Sauce."

MRS. H. VAN EVRA.

COCOANUT PUDDING.

Yolks of two eggs, one pint milk, one-half cup sugar, one tablespoon corn starch, one cocoanut grated. Bake one-half hour. Beat the whites with a little powdered sugar, then pour over pudding and brown.

MRS. D. S. MORRELL.

LEMON CREAM PUDDING.

Beat yolks of four eggs with four tablespoons of sugar. Add juice and grated rind of one lemon and two tablespoons hot water. Simmer until thickened. Remove from fire. Stir in whites of four eggs beaten to a stiff froth with two tablespoons sugar. Stir in the whites by tablespoons, beating some time after all are added.

MRS. H. D. WALKER.

SAGO AND APPLE PUDDING.

Pare apples and punch out the cores. Fill holes with cinnamon and sugar, using two teaspoons of cinnamon to a cup of sugar. Put in pan a heaping tablespoon of sago to each apple. Put in the apples, fill the pan (nearly) with water and bake one and one-half hours.

MRS. H. D. W.

USING PETTIT'S CIDER AND FRUIT PRESERVATIVE.

SNOW PUDDING, No. 1.

Whites of five eggs beaten very stiff, one-half box of gelatine soaked in warm water, juice of one lemon, one cup powdered sugar. Add sugar to eggs, and having put gelatine and lemon juice through a strainer, beat gradually into eggs. Put in mould. Served with cream or custard.   CLARA T. VAN STEENBERGH.

SNOW PUDDING, No. 2.

One pint of boiling water, three tablespoons corn starch dissolved in cold water, whites of three eggs thoroughly beaten, a little salt. Stir corn starch into water until clear. Add the whites with two tablespoons of sugar. Remove from fire when thoroughly mixed. Flavor and pour in mould. Serve with custard No. 1.
   MRS. E. M'KINSTRY.

GRAHAM PUDDING.

A scant cup of butter, one-half cup of molasses, one cup sweet milk, one and one-half cup graham flour, one teaspoon soda, one egg, one cup seeded raisins, one teaspoon each of cloves, cinnamon and nutmeg. Steam two and one-half hours. Serve with sauce No. 1.   MRS. C. G. PETTIT.

SUET PUDDING, No. 1.

One cup of suet, one-half cup molasses, one cup sweet milk, one cup seeded raisins, one tablespoon ginger, one teaspoon cream tartar, one-half teaspoon soda, flour to make a stiff batter. Boil two hours.   MRS. J. C. M'C.

SUET PUDDING, No. 2.

One cup of suet, one cup molasses, three cups of flour, one and one-half cups milk, one and one-half cups of seeded raisins, one cup currants, three tablespoons baking powder. Steam three hours in pudding tin. If wanted richer, add more fruit. Serve with wine sauce.   CLARA T. VAN STEENBERGH.

TRY PRESERVING YOUR FRUIT WITHOUT HEAT.

TAPIOCA CREAM OR FRENCH CUSTARD.

Four tablespoons tapioca soaked over night in water enough to cover. Beat yolks of three eggs and two-thirds of a cup of sugar. Mix with tapioca after draining. Heat one quart milk, put in eggs, sugar and tapioca. Let boil until thick as custard Salt and flavor. Use whites of eggs for meringue, allowing two tablespoons of sugar to one egg. Serve cold. MRS. D. S. READ.

SIMPLE RICE PUDDING.

One cup of rice boiled in water until nearly soft, drain, and add milk instead. When quite soft, add yolks of four eggs and four tablespoons sugar, then beat whites with same quantity of sugar and any flavor you wish. Pour on top of pudding, and set in oven long enough to brown slightly. MRS. E. F. S.

QUEEN'S PUDDING.

One pint of bread crumbs, one quart milk, one cup sugar, grated rind of one lemon, one teaspoon lemon extract, small piece of butter, pinch of salt. Bake in good oven, then spread a layer of jam over the top and cover with a meringue made with whites of two eggs. To be eaten hot or cold. H. V. D.

CHOCOLATE PUDDING.

One quart of milk. While boiling, add one and one-half ounces of chocolate dissolved in milk. When nearly cold stir in beaten yolks of six eggs, with four tablespoons of sugar. Flavor with vanilla. Bake like custard. Beat the whites of the eggs with six tablespoons of sugar. Pour over pudding. Bake three minutes. To be eaten cold. MRS. M. L. SMITH.

PEACH PUDDING.

Slice a quart of peaches in a pudding dish, put in a small piece of butter. Take yolks of two eggs, one tablespoon of corn starch, one pint of sweet milk and one cup of sugar. Let it come to a boil, and pour over the peaches. Then bake. When done, beat the whites to a stiff froth, sweeten and pour over the top, return to the oven and brown. To be eaten cold or hot. MRS. M. L. S.

USING PETTIT'S CIDER AND FRUIT PRESERVATIVE.

COTTAGE PUDDING.

One cup of sugar, one cup sweet milk, one egg, three tablespoons melted butter, three teaspoons baking powder, one pint of flour. Bake and serve hot with wine sauce.   MARTHA A. RICE.

JELLY PUDDING.

One cup pearl tapioca, soaked over night in one and one-half pints of water. Cook one hour, then add salt, half cup of sugar, one tumbler of jelly, stir till dissolved and set it on ice. Serve with "milk sauce."   CONTRIBUTED.

ECLAIR PUDDING.

Four eggs, one cup sugar, one cup flour, one teaspoon of baking powder. Bake this. When baked, spread with the following icing: Icing—The white of one egg, one-half cup of sugar, two tablespoons grated chocolate. Boil until thick and smooth. Just before serving pudding, split and fill with the following custard: One pint milk, a little salt, yolks of three eggs, one-half cup sugar, two tablespoons corn starch. Flavor with vanilla.
  FLORENCE M. SPRAKER.

DIXIE PUDDING.

One quart of milk, one pint bread crumbs, one pound sugar, six or four eggs, two small or one large lemon. Separate the whites from the yolks, and add to the yolks four tablespoons of sugar. Then add the bread crumbs and milk with the grated rind of the lemon and bake. Beat the whites, sugar and lemon juice together until light. When the pudding is nearly cold, cover with the icing and bake a light brown.   CONTRIBUTED.

RICE PUDDING.

One quart of milk, four tablespoons of rice, butter size of half an egg, one half cup sugar, a little salt. Bake slowly two hours.
  MRS. M. L. SMITH.

TRY PRESERVING YOUR FRUIT WITHOUT HEAT.

BREAD PUDDING.

Spread with butter two slices of bread, cut in dice. Prepare a custard of one quart milk, four eggs, sugar to taste, nutmeg. Pour over bread, bake until custard is done. Serve with hard sauce, with or without wine. MRS. D. S READ.

TIPSY PARSON.

Blanch one pound of almonds by pouring on boiling water. When cold they will slip out of skins. Stick them in a sponge cake. Pour over cake one cup sherry wine. Have ready a custard and pour over the cake. Prepare just before serving.
MRS. D. S. READ.

GERMAN TOAST.

Take stale baker's bread sliced, one pint sweet milk. Beat one egg in milk. Dip in the bread about one hour before using. Lay on moulding board to dry. When ready to be served bake on a pancake griddle. The sauce—one egg, three-quarters of a cup of sugar, one-half cup butter, wine glass sherry wine. Mix butter and sugar. Add yolk beaten. Add sherry and beaten whites of eggs. Serve on bread hot. MISS O. WAGNER.

INDIAN PUDDING.

Two tablespoons of Indian meal, one tablespoon wheat flour. Mix with a little cold milk, then stir into one quart of boiling milk. Add a little salt and boil twenty minutes. When cold, beat two eggs, a cup of sugar. Add spice, and bake three quarters of an hour. A. C. G.

HAMILTON PUDDING.

Two eggs, two tablespoons sugar, one-half cup butter, one cup milk, one cup chopped raisins, two cups flour, three teaspoons baking powder. Melt butter and add sugar. Beat eggs thoroughly and add the milk. Flour the raisins. Put baking powder in flour Steam in large cups one hour. Wine sauce.
MRS. W. N. S.

USING PETTIT'S CIDER AND FRUIT PRESERVATIVE.

INDIAN BAKED PUDDING.

One quart sweet milk, butter size of butternut, three eggs well beaten, one teacup Indian meal, one-half cup seeded raisins, two-thirds of a cup of sugar. Scald the milk and stir in the meal while boiling, then let it stand until warm. Stir all together and bake one and one-half hours.   MRS. G. W. VAN VLACK.

FIG PUDDING.

One-half lb. of beef suet chopped very fine, one and one-half pints bread crumbs rolled very fine, three-quarters lb. fresh figs chopped very fine, one whole grated nutmeg, two teaspoons cinnamon, one wine glass good sherry wine, one-half teacup sugar, yolks of four eggs, one teacup sweet milk, one teacup sifted flour, one teaspoon baking powder in the flour. Beat all well together and steam three hours.

SAUCE FOR FIG PUDDING.

Whites of four eggs, leave the yolks for pudding; one teacup powdered sugar, wine glass good sherry, beat well and have soft and pour over pudding before serving.

MRS. G. W. VAN V.

CRACKER PUDDING.

Seven Boston crackers rolled very fine, three pints of milk, three eggs well beaten, one and one-half cups sugar, one-half cup butter, one-half cup seeded raisins, one-half teaspoon nutmeg, one-half teaspoon cinnamon, pinch of salt. Mix the whole in the dish to be baked in. Bake the day before in a moderate oven, four to five hours. Serve cold with cream which is whipped, *without* sugar.

MRS. G. W. VAN V.

CORN STARCH PUDDING.

Two rounded tablespoons corn starch, wet to a smooth paste with water, add to this two-thirds pint boiling water, and cook in a double boiler until corn starch boils and thickens; remove and mix with the whites of two eggs stiffly beaten. Turn in a mould to harden.

TRY PRESERVING YOUR FRUIT WITHOUT HEAT.

SAUCE FOR PUDDING.

Beat the yolks of the eggs well, add a scant cup of sugar, one cup of milk, cook in a double boiler till thick as cream, and add flavoring. MRS. W. N. S.

PRUNE PUDDING.

Stew one lb. prunes, till soft, remove pits, and beat up fine with a fork. Beat the white of one egg stiff, and add to one pint cream, after it has been whipped to a froth, and a heaping tablespoon of sugar stirred in. Mix all with prunes, put in dish and bake twenty minutes. MRS. E. M'K.

SAUCE No. 1.

Beat together one cup of sugar and one half cup of butter, until creamy; add one tablespoon flour, and stir again. Just before serving set on stove and stir in three-quarters pint of boiling water, stirring until it thickens. MRS. C. G. P.

MILK SAUCE,

One cup of sugar, one egg, one pint of milk, one tablespoon flour, cook five minutes or until done. COX.

SAUCE FOR VELVET PUDDING.

Yolks of two eggs, one cup white sugar, one tablespoon of butter. Beat eggs and all the other ingredients well and add one cup boiling milk, then place it over the fire and let it come to a boiling heat. Flavor with vanilla. A. C. G.

CREAMY SAUCE.

One half cup butter, one cup powdered sugar, four tablespoons of cream or milk, four tablespoons of wine, or four additional spoons of milk. Beat butter to a cream, add sugar and milk gradually beating till very light. Place bowl in which sauce has been made in a basin of boiling water, stir a few minutes till smooth. The last to be done just before serving. MRS. D. S. R.

USING PETTIT'S CIDER AND FRUIT PRESERVATIVE.

CREAM SAUCE, (COLD.)

One pint cream, four tablespoons sugar, nutmeg or vanilla. Stir until sugar is dissolved.   MRS. D. S. R.

FOAM SAUCE.

One cup of sugar, two-thirds cup butter, one tablespoon of flour. Add one spoonful of hot water, enough to enable you to beat light. When ready to serve, add three gills boiling water, beating at the time. Do not cook. One half wine glass of brandy added at the last will make a good brandy sauce.   MRS. D. S. R.

HARD SAUCE.

One half cup butter, one and one-half cup powdered sugar. Add sugar gradually and beat till very light. Add wine glass of sherry wine with a little nutmeg.   MRS. D. S. R.

SAUCE FOR DUMPLINGS.

One cup molasses, one cup light brown sugar, one cup boiling water, butter size of an egg, nutmeg to taste.' Boil and thicken with a little flour.   MISS O. WAGNER.

PUDDING SAUCE FOR THREE PEOPLE.

One egg well beaten, one-half cup of sugar, add three tablespoons hot milk, stir well. Make in a bowl and set in the top of teakettle, let it stand until ready to serve, without stirring, then add two teaspoons wine or brandy. Make just before serving.

    MRS. W. N. S.

TRY PRESERVING YOUR FRUIT WITHOUT HEAT.

ICES, ICE CREAMS, JELLIES, ETC.

LEMON ICE.

To one quart of water add one lb. sugar, the juice of four lemons and one orange. Let the sugar dissolve thoroughly, strain and freeze. MRS. D. S. MORRELL.

If desired, the well-beaten whites of two eggs can be added just before freezing.

FRUIT ICES.

These are made by taking one quart of any desired fruit, raw or canned, cut in *very* small slices or pieces: add one quart water, and about three-fourths lb. sugar, according to acidity of fruit. The beaten white of one egg added just before freezing, is an improvement. "E."

LEMON SHERBET.

Soak one tablespoon of gelatine in one cup water till soft, add one cup boiling water to dissolve. When cool, strain, add one lb. sugar, one quart cold water, and the juice of four or five lemons. Freeze.

ORANGE SHERBET.

To the juice of ten large oranges take one quart water and one lb. sugar. Soak one large tablespoon of gelatine in a little water, adding when soft half a cup of boiling water; strain and cool, mix with the other ingredients, and freeze.

FRUIT FRAPPÉE.

Line a mold with ice cream. Put fresh sliced fruit or berries in the centre, fill up the mold with ice cream, cover very closely, and pack in ice and salt for about half an hour.

USING PETTIT'S CIDER AND FRUIT PRESERVATIVE.

ICE CREAM.

For one gallon of ice cream, take two quarts of rich milk, one quart of cream, one pound and a quarter of sugar, (granulated or white coffee sugar,) and full one-third of a box of Cox's gelatine. Let the gelatine soak for half an hour, or until soft, in one quart of the milk, then put on the range, but not where very hot. Stir constantly until quite dissolved, then add the sugar, and do not cease stirring until that has also dissolved, when strain directly into the freezer, and add the other quart of milk. If in haste, the freezer can be set in a pail of cold water, and the milk kept stirred for a few minutes; otherwise stand in a cool place, first adding one large tablespoonful of extract of vanilla. When ready to freeze, stir in the cream. MRS. EMELINE F. SMITH.

WHITE ICE CREAM.

Take two quarts cream and one quart milk; beat together one pound of sugar, and the whites of two eggs, mix with the cream, and whip with egg-beater until frothed; add milk, lemon flavor, and freeze.

STRAWBERRY ICE CREAM.

Put one pound of granulated sugar over one quart strawberries, and let stand for an hour. Then add one quart of sweet cream and freeze. Peaches sliced small can be used instead of strawberries, made in the same manner. MISS VENETTE STAFFORD.

STRAWBERRY CREAM.

One-half box of gelatine dissolved in one-half cup of water; when soft, add one cup of boiling water, and put aside to cool. Mash together one quart strawberries and one cup powdered sugar, let stand one hour, strain berries and add to gelatine; place pail in pan of ice water and beat until it thickens; stir in one pint whipped cream. Turn into mould to cool. MRS. N. S. B.

TRY PRESERVING YOUR FRUIT WITHOUT HEAT,

BISCUIT GLACÉ.

Yolks of four eggs beaten, sweetened and flavored to taste. Two quarts cream *after* it is beaten and sweetened. Put yolks in pan with cream on top; set in ice and salt for two hours, when it will be sufficiently frozen. MRS. L. W. FROST.

CHARLOTTE RUSSE.

One quart of cream whipped; sweeten and flavor with vanilla. First dissolve one-half box of gelatine in two-thirds pint of water, strain gelatine, and stir slowly into the cream while warm. Add a small pinch of salt. Let cream stand until it commences to thicken, then stir thoroughly and turn into tins lined with sponge cake. This will serve sixteen people. MRS. N. S. B.

SPANISH CREAM.

One quart of cream, one cup powdered sugar, one tablespoon of gelatine soaked in three tablespoons of water, beat in whites of three eggs, then stir in beaten cream. Turn in mould and set away to cool. C. T. V. S.

BAVARIAN CREAM.

One quart sweet cream, yolks of four eggs, one half box gelatine, one teacup sugar, vanilla or almond to taste. Soak gelatine in a little cold water one hour, stir in half the cream hot, beat yolks with sugar and add, heat till it begins to thicken. When cool stir in remainder of cream beaten to a froth, a spoonful at a time, beating till like sponge cake mixture. Turn in mould and set on ice. May be made with half milk. MRS. D. S. R.

SPANISH CREAM, No. 2.

Dissolve one-half box Cox's gelatine in one pint cold milk, scald another pint of milk, and pour over when gelatine is dissolved. Beat yolks of two eggs with one cup sugar, and stir in milk, cook ten minutes, then add the whites of eggs beaten stiff, stir briskly a few minutes, and then pour in mould and stand away to harden. Eat with cream or lemon sauce.

USING PETTIT'S CIDER AND FRUIT PRESERVATIVE.

LEMON SAUCE.

The juice of one lemon, one large cup water, one-half tea-cup sugar. Let this come to a boil. Beat the yolks of two eggs light, into which pour the boiling liquid, stirring hard. Set back on stove, let it come to a boil again, stirring all the time. Pour in sauce dish and stand away to cool. Beat the whites of the eggs very stiff, with three tablespoons powdered sugar, and put on top of sauce.

MRS. E. F. S.

FLOATING ISLAND.

The whites of four eggs, four tablespoons of currant jelly, four tablespoons powdered sugar. Beat all together until very light and stiff. Flavor with vanilla. Serve with cream. MRS. B.

FOR A DESSERT.

Line a large dish with sponge cake, thickly spread with jelly or marmalade. Then fill the dish with the whips.

WHIPS.

Sweeten one pint of cream, add a glass of wine. Stand in a cool place while you beat the whites of four eggs to a stiff froth, add these to the cream, stirring rapidly, and pour in the dish.

MRS. J. C. M'C.

WINE JELLY.

One box of Cox's gelatine, pour over it one pint cold water, let it stand ten minutes, then add one quart boiling water, one and one-half pounds sugar, mix well, add a little stick of cinnamon, if desired. When nearly cold, add one pint wine, a wine-glass of brandy; strain through a fine cloth into moulds. MRS. J. C. M'C.

LEMON JELLY.

Dissolve one-half box of gelatine in one cup cold water, grate two and one-half lemons, take off the thick skin, and grate the pulp. Put three cups of sugar and three cups water in a kettle, let it boil a few minutes, then add the pulp, the grated rind, and dissolve gelatine, and one tablespoon of vinegar, and let boil a moment longer. Strain into mould. M. A. R.

TRY PRESERVING YOUR FRUIT WITHOUT HEAT,

PHILADELPHIA JELLY.

Over three-quarters of a box of gelatine, pour one-half pint cold water, and let it stand for ten minutes, then add a half pint of boiling water. Squeeze the juice of two lemons, and add with the sugar to the gelatine while hot. Strain and let it stand until it begins to thicken, then stir in two oranges and two bananas sliced, and turn into mould to harden. Eat with cream. Wine jelly can be used instead of lemon jelly.   MRS. B.

CIDER JELLY.

Two-thirds of a box of gelatine, two coffee cups granulated sugar, one-half pint cold water, one-half pint cider, one pint boiling water, juice of one lemon, pinch of cinnamon. Put gelatine to soak in the cold water one hour, have ready the sugar, cinnamon and lemon juice, add gelatine, then the boiling water, and lastly the cider, adding two tablespoons brandy.   CON.

QUICK CHARLOTTE RUSSE.

One tea cup cream, one teaspoon gelatine dissolved in a very little warm water; beat cream thick and sweeten and flavor to taste; add gelatine and pour into dish lined with lady fingers, or slices of sponge cake. Let the gelatine cool, and turn into the cream while beating it.   MRS. W. N. S.

ORANGE CHARLOTTE.

One third box of gelatine, one-third cup of cold water, one-third cup boiling water, one cup sugar, juice of one lemon, one cup of orange juice and pulp, whites of three eggs. Line mould with lady fingers. One pint of cream may be used in place of eggs. Other fruits can be used.   MRS. W. N. S.

APPLE COMPOTE.

Pare and core eight apples, leaving whole. Make a syrup of three fourths pound of sugar, to one pound of fruit; when it boils put in the fruit and boil till clear; place fruit in a glass bowl. Dissolve half a box of gelatine in one-half cup of hot water, and stir briskly into the syrup, having first taken it from the fire; strain over apples, and set in a cool place.   CON.

USING PETTIT'S CIDER AND FRUIT PRESERVATIVE.

STRAWBERRY CREAM.

One half cup gelatine dissolved in half cup water, when soft add one-half cup boiling water, put aside to cool; one quart straw-strawberries, one pint cream, one cup powdered sugar. Mash berries and sugar together, let stand one hour. Whip the cream, strain berries and geletine. Place pail in pan of ice water and beat till it thickens; stir in whipped cream, and turn into molds to cool. MRS. N. S. BRUMLEY.

CAKES.

GENERAL DIRECTIONS.

In preparing the materials for cake-making, the flour and sugar should be carefully sifted before weighing or measuring. If the butter is slightly softened and beaten with a fork before putting it with the sugar, they will mix more easily. If eggs are to be beaten separately, no speck of the yolk should be allowed to mix with the whites. Baking powder should always be mixed with the flour. If soda and cream tartar are used, sift the latter into the flour, and dissolve the soda in the milk. If fruit is used, seed raisins and chop a little, wash currants carefully and dry, slice citron very thin. A little of the flour should be saved to mix with the fruit, which should be added last of all.

The following table will be of use where scales are not at hand :
One quart of flour, sifted and well heaped, weighs   one pound.
Four teacups sifted flour, even full, weigh .   .   . "   "
One pint soft butter, well packed, weighs .   .   . "   "
Two and three-quarters teacups powdered sugar weigh "   "
Two teacups granulated sugar weigh .   .   . "   "
Two teacups, heaped, best coffee sugar, weigh .   "   "
Two and a half teacups best brown sugar weigh .   "   "
Two tablespoons, well heaped, of flour, weigh   . one ounce.
Soft butter, size of an egg, weighs   .   .   .   . two ounces.
One wine glass, common size, equals four tablespoons or two fluid ounces.
A common sized tumbler or teacup holds half a pint.

TRY PRESERVING YOUR FRUIT WITHOUT HEAT,

ANGEL'S FOOD.

Use for measuring, a large cup or tumbler holding three-fourths of a pint, and let the measure be only level full. Sift one cup of flour four times, then measure, (it will have increased in bulk,) add one teaspoonful cream tartar and sift again; one cup and a half granulated sugar, sift and measure again: the whites of eleven eggs beaten to a very stiff froth before adding sugar, and one teaspoon vanilla, then the flour lightly stirred in. Put in ungreased and very clean pan, set in moderate oven, which should not be opened for fifteen minutes. Bake for forty minutes. Try with broom splint, and let it remain a few minutes longer if not quite baked. Turn pan upside down to cool, standing edges on something to prevent it from resting down on table.

ANGEL'S FOOD, No. 2.

Whites of eleven eggs beaten very light, one-half pound pulverized sugar, one-fourth pound flour, one teaspoon lemon essence, one teaspoon cream tartar. Sift flour and sugar several times before using. Bake in tunnel dish without paper or greasing.

MISS O. M. WAGNER.

DELICATE CAKE.

Two cups sugar, one-half cup butter, two-thirds cup milk, two and one-half cups flour, two teaspoons baking powder, whites of eight eggs. Flavor to taste.   MRS. L. W. FROST.

CORNSTARCH CAKES.

Two cups pulverized sugar, one scant cup butter, one-half cup milk, six eggs beaten separately, one paper corn starch, two teaspoons baking powder. Bake in patty pan tins.

MRS. A. J. READ.

SUNSHINE CAKE.

Whites of ten eggs, yolks of seven, one tumbler of flour, one and a half tumblers of granulated sugar, one teaspoon cream tartar, juice and grated rind of one lemon, one-half teaspoon of ammonia, (aqua ammonia will answer.) Beat the yolks and one-half tumbler of sugar very light. Beat the whites of the eggs to a stiff froth, stirring in lightly the remainder of the sugar. Add the beaten yolks and sugar, the lemon also, and stir in the flour lightly, adding the ammonia last. Sift the sugar once before measuring. Sift the flour three times and measure. Then add the cream tartar to it and sift again. Bake in an ungreased pan as in Angel's Food, and when baked turn the pan upside down until cake is cool. CON.

LADY'S CAKE.

One-half cup butter, one and one-half cups sugar, two cups flour, one cup (scant) sweet milk, one teaspoon cream tartar, one-half teaspoon soda, whites of four eggs well beaten. Flavor with peach or almond. MRS. H. D. WALKER.

SILVER CAKE.

Two cups sugar, two and one-half cups flour, one-half cup butter, three-fourths cup sweet milk, one-half teaspoonful soda dissolved in milk, whites of eight eggs, one teaspoonful cream tartar. Stir butter and sugar together, then add the whites beaten to a stiff froth, then the milk. After stirring this well, add the cream tartar dry. Bake half an hour. MRS. C. H. BURBECK.

SPONGE CAKE.

Six eggs, one and one-half cups sugar, one and one-half cups flour, one tablespoon ice water or lemon juice, one heaped teaspoon baking powder. Beat yolks and sugar till very light. Beat whites to stiff froth, adding last carefully. This makes a good-sized loaf. For smaller, use four eggs, one cup each of sugar and flour, same amount of water and baking powder.

MRS. D. S. READ.

SPONGE CAKE, No. 2.

Yolks of three eggs beaten with one cup of sugar very thoroughly. Add one-half cup of water, one good teaspoon of baking powder, one and one-half cups of flour. Beat the whites to a stiff froth and add just before putting in the oven. MRS. H. D. W.

TRY PRESERVING YOUR FRUIT WITHOUT HEAT,

DELICATE CAKE.

One cup sugar, one-half cup butter, one-half cup milk, one and one half cups flour, whites of four eggs, one teaspoon baking powder.
            MRS. N. S. BRUMLEY.

CUP CAKE.

One cup butter, two cups sugar, three cups flour, one cup milk four eggs, two teaspoons baking powder. Bake in loaf or layers or add spice and raisins for spice cake, with tablespoon of molasses.
            MRS. D. S. R.

POUND CAKE, OLD RECEIPT.

Three-quarters pound of butter, beaten to a cream, one pound sugar, ten eggs, whites and yolks beaten separately, one wine glass brandy, flavor with nutmeg, one pound flour. Beat for half an hour, bake in slow oven for nearly an hour. Try with broom splint; if it comes out clean the cake is done.   MRS. E. F. S.

CHEAP POUND CAKE.

One cup sugar, one-half cup butter, three eggs, five tablespoons sweet milk, one cup flour, two teaspoons baking powder.
            MRS. D. S. R.

COCOANUT CAKE.

Three cups sugar, three quarters cup butter, one cup sweet milk, whites of six eggs, three and one half cups flour, one teaspoon soda, two of cream tartar, one of salt, and the grated meat of one cocoanut.   MRS. E. F. S.

NUT CAKE.

Two cups sugar, half cup butter, half cup milk, two cups flour, whites of five eggs, one teaspoon baking powder, one coffee cup nut pits; add the beaten whites last or after part of flour has been put in.   MRS. C. G. PETTIT.

CLAY CAKE.

One pound of sugar, half pound of butter, six eggs, three teaspoons baking powder, half pint sweet milk, one pound of flour; flavor. Bake in loaf or layers.   MRS. E. F. S.

USING PETTIT'S CIDER AND FRUIT PRESERVATIVE.

FIG FILLING, FOR CAKE.

One cup seeded raisins, half pound figs, both chopped. Put in pan with one cup sugar and half cup hot water, boil till smooth and thick, stirring often. Set off to cool, then spread on cake ; it is enough for two layers.
H. B S.

CLARK CAKE.

Two cups sugar, three-quarters cup butter, one cup milk, whites of six eggs, three heaping teaspoons baking powder, three cups of flour : flavor.
MRS. J. N. SNELL.

OLD GOLD CAKE.

Six ounces sugar, six ounces flour, three ounces butter, yolks of six eggs, one and one-half teaspoons baking powder, one-third cup milk. Flavor with nutmeg and add three quarters cup of currants.
EMELINE.

SOFT JUMBLE CAKE.

Two coffee cups sugar and four eggs beaten together twenty minutes ; add one cup butter beaten to a cream, three teaspoonfuls baking powder, one cup milk and three cups flour.
MRS. E. F. S.

PUFF CAKE.

One cup butter, three cups sugar, four cups flour, one cup milk, five eggs, one teaspoon soda, two teaspoons cream tartar. Dissolve soda in milk, and sift cream tartar with flour. It is very nice with grated rind and juice of lemon. Can be baked in large flat pan and cut in diamonds, or baked in layers.
MRS. JACOB H. NELLIS.

MINNEHAHA CAKE.

Two cups sugar, half cup butter, one cup milk, three cups flour, three eggs, two teaspoons baking powder. For filling, one teacup sugar with a very little water boiled together until brittle when dropped in water. Remove from stove and stir in quickly the white of a well beaten egg, two cups chopped raisins, or one cup of raisins and one cup of hickory nuts.
MRS. W. BULLOCK.

TRY PRESERVING YOUR FRUIT WITHOUT HEAT,

FEATHER CAKE.

One tablespoon butter, one cup sugar, one cup milk, two cups flour, three teaspoons baking powder, one egg.   MRS. D. S. R.

SANDWICH CAKE.

Two cups of sugar, three-quarters cup of butter, one cup sweet milk, three eggs, two and a half cups flour, three teaspoons of baking powder. Take out four tablespoons of dough, add one-half cup of molasses, half cup of flour, one cup of chopped raisins, half teaspoon of nutmeg, cinnamon and cloves. Put together with jelly.   MRS. G. W. GOODRICH.

CHOCOLATE CAKE, No. 1.

One cup grated chocolate, one cup sugar, one cup milk, one egg, butter size of hickory nut, one teaspoon vanilla, one cup flour, one teaspoon soda. Cook chocolate with yolk of egg and half cup of milk, then add remainder of milk, butter and flour. Bake in two layers and put together with frosting.

MRS. G. H. WATSON.

CHOCOLATE CAKE, No. 2.

Three eggs, three-quarters cup butter, two cups sugar, two cups flour, (scant,) one cup milk, four squares chocolate, grated, one small teaspoon soda, two small teaspoons cream tartar. Beat sugar and butter together, add yolks of eggs. Sift soda and cream tartar with the flour. Stir chocolate into milk, add flour, chocolate and milk. Beat whites of eggs, add last. Bake three-quarters of an hour in a moderate oven. This must be made carefully. Can be baked in two loaves, or three layers and put an icing of confectioner's sugar between.   MISS MANNY.

CHOCOLATE CAKE, No. 3.

Four eggs, two cups sugar, one cup butter, one cup milk, three cups flour, three teaspoons baking powder. Filling, half cup grated chocolate, one and one-half cups pulverized sugar, half cup milk. Let boil till quite thick, stirring all the time. Just before

USING PETTIT'S CIDER AND FRUIT PRESERVATIVE.

removing from the fire, add one egg well beaten; when cold flavor with vanilla. MRS. A. J. R.

ICE CREAM CAKE.

Whites of eight eggs, one cup sweet milk, one cup butter, two cups sugar, two cups flour, two teaspoonfuls baking powder mixed with the flour, one cup cornstarch. Beat butter and sugar to a cream, add milk, then flour and cornstarch, then whites of eggs beaten very light. Bake in layers. Icing—Whites of four eggs beaten very light, four cups sugar. Pour half pint boiling water over the sugar and boil until clear and will string from the spoon. Pour the boiling syrup over the whites of eggs and beat until cold and creamy. Flavor with lemon or vanilla.

MRS. W. N. SCHOLL.
CREAM CAKE.

Two cups sugar, half cup butter, one cup milk, two heaping cups flour, whites of three eggs, two teaspoons baking powder. Cream—Yolks of two eggs, two-thirds cup milk, one tablespoon flour or cornstarch, a little salt and a little sugar. Flavor with lemon or vanilla. MISS M. A. RICE.

LEMON JELLY CAKE.

Four eggs, two cups sugar, two-thirds cup butter, two thirds cup milk, two cups flour, one teaspoon baking powder. Jelly—One grated lemon, one cup sugar, one egg, two tablespoons hot water, butter size of walnut. Boil till thick. MRS. A. J. R.

ORANGE CAKE.

Two teacups sugar, two cups flour, half cup cold water, five eggs, two teaspoons baking powder, juice and a very little of the grated rind of an orange. Bake in layers, (three) put between them icing, upon which lay thin slices of orange; also on top of cake. Icing—White of one egg, one tablespoon of water, stir in confectioner's sugar until thick enough not to run. MRS. E. F. S.

FILLING FOR CHARLOTTE RUSSE CAKE.

Dissolve one tablespoon gelatine in a very little hot water, and add to one cup sweet cream, sweetened and flavored with vanilla

TRY PRESERVING YOUR FRUIT WITHOUT HEAT.

and whipped to a stiff froth. Put between layers and on top of any layer cake.
MRS. G. H. W.

LEMON CAKE.

Five eggs, whites and yolks beaten separately, one cup butter, one and one-half cups sugar, four teaspoonfuls milk, two small teaspoonfuls baking powder, two and one-half cups flour. Bake in layers. Lemon frosting—One cup sugar, two tablespoonfuls butter, two eggs, juice of two lemons. Boil all together until the consistency of jelly.
MRS. J. C. M'C.

ENGLISH WALNUT CAKE.

Whites of five eggs, one and one-half cups sugar, one half cup butter, one cup milk, three cups flour, two teaspoons baking powder. Bake in three layers, putting between icing made of confectioner's sugar, and English walnut meats broken fine. Put icing on top with whole meats laid over thickly.
MRS. E. M'K.

FIG CAKE.

One cup butter, two cups sugar, one cup milk, three cups flour, whites of six eggs, two and one-half teaspoons baking powder. For filling, one-half pound figs, one-half pound raisins, one cup sugar, one cup warm water. Chop figs and raisins very fine; put in sugar and water, and boil till quite thick.
MRS. J. N. S.

HICKORY CAKE.

One pound sugar, one pound flour, one half pound butter, four eggs, one teacup sweet milk, three teaspoons baking powder; flavoring of vanilla, one large cup stoned raisins, one cup hickory-nut meats.
MRS. E. F. S.

FRUIT CAKE.

Four pounds of currants, three pounds of raisins, one pound citron, one pound flour, one pound butter, one and one-half pounds sugar, one gill brandy, one gill molasses, ten eggs. Bake in four quart pan four hours, in slow oven.
MRS. T. W. BINGHAM.

USING PETTIT'S CIDER AND FRUIT PRESERVATIVE.

TOLEDO BREAD CAKE.

One pint bread dough, one cup butter, two cups brown sugar, four eggs, one wine-glass brandy, one teaspoon soda in brandy; one nutmeg, one-half teaspoon cinnamon, two cups seeded raisins, one cup flour. MRS. C. H. WHITAKER.

MY CAKE.

Two cups brown sugar, one cup sour milk, two cups flour, one-half cup butter, two eggs, one teaspoon soda, two teaspoons cream tartar. Put both soda and cream tartar in the milk the last thing. Fruit and spices to taste. MRS. G. W. GEORTNER.

COFFEE CAKE.

One coffee cup molasses, one of brown sugar, three-fourths of butter, one of cold coffee, two eggs, two even teaspoons soda, four of cream tartar, one large teaspoon each of cinnamon and cloves, one grated nutmeg, three and one-half coffee cups flour, one pound seeded raisins. MRS. E. F. S.

EGGLESS CAKE.

One cup sugar, one-half cup molasses, two tablespoons butter, one cup sweet milk, one cup seeded and chopped raisins, two teaspoons soda, cloves, cinnamon and nutmeg of each an even teaspoonful, two and one-half cups of flour. MRS. C. G. P.

CAKE WITHOUT EGGS.

One small cup butter, two of sugar, four of flour, two full teaspoons baking powder, one teaspoon cinnamon, one-half teaspoon cloves. Rub all together until very fine. One and one-half cups milk, one cup chopped raisins. Be sure to stir well together. This makes two loaves. MRS. H. D. W.

MOLASSES CAKE, No. 1.

One cup molasses, one-half cup brown sugar, one-half cup butter, one teaspoon soda dissolved in one cup of boiling water, one egg, two cups of flour. E. M'K.

TRY PRESERVING YOUR FRUIT WITHOUT HEAT,

BOSTON MOLASSES CAKE, NO. 2.

Three cups flour, one cup each of sour milk, sugar and molasses, two-thirds butter, two eggs, one teaspoon soda. Spice to taste. This makes two loaves.   MRS. G. W. GEORTNER.

SOFT MOLASSES CAKE, No. 1.

One cup molasses, one brown sugar, one sour milk, four tablespoons lard, two teaspoons soda, one salt, ginger and cinnamon to taste; mix soft, drop with spoon.   ANNE BULLOCK.

SOFT MOLASSES CAKE, No. 2.

One cup of butter, one-half brown sugar, one molasses, two eggs, one teaspoon soda dissolved in one-half cup sour milk, or sweet milk can be used. Add flour enough to make a batter not too stiff; ginger or spice may be added, also fruit.   MRS. J. H. N.

MOLASSES CAKE, No. 3.

One cup molasses, one sour cream or milk, two flour, one egg, one teaspoon soda, ginger and pinch of salt. Bake in two pie tins. To be eaten hot.   MRS. W. B.

MOLASSES COOKIES.

Two cups of molasses, eight tablespoons lard, one-half cup water, three teaspoons soda, one teaspoon alum. Take one-half of the water, and put in the soda, and the other one-half put the alum in. Add the alum in water last, mix soft: add a little cinnamon, if you choose.   MRS. HARRIET TAYLOR.

DROP CAKES.

Two eggs, one cup sugar, one molasses, twelve tablespoons melted butter, one teaspoon soda, one teaspoon alum, three-fourths cup sour milk, cloves, cinnamon and ginger to taste, four cups flour.   MRS. L. C.

CRULLERS, No. 1.

One coffee cup sugar, one egg, two tablespoons butter, three teaspoons baking powder, one quart of flour, mixed with sweet milk.   MRS. FRASIER SPEAKER.

USING PETTIT'S CIDER AND FRUIT PRESERVATIVE.

CRULLERS. No. 2.

One cup sugar, one sweet milk, one egg, two teaspoons baking powder, a little nutmeg; mix as soft as you can roll out, fry in hot lard.　　　　　　　　　　　　　　　　　　　　　　　　S. A. R.

CRULLERS, No. 3.

One quart flour, three teaspoons baking powder, one and one-half tablespoons melted lard rubbed in flour, two cups light brown sugar, two eggs, a little nutmeg, enough milk to make soft enough to roll out, fry in hot lard.　　　　　　　　　　　　　O. M. WAGNER.

CRULLERS, No. 4.

Two cups sugar, one sour milk, two tablespoons sour cream, or one and one-half of melted butter, five eggs, teaspoon soda, nutmeg.
　　　　　　　　　　　　　　　　　　　　　　　　MRS. JOHN VOSBURG.

FRIED CAKES.

Three eggs, one and one-half cups sugar, four tablespoons melted lard, one cup of sweet milk, three heaping teaspoons baking powder, one even teaspoon of salt, mix very soft.　　　　　E. M'K.

JUMBLES, No. 1.

Four eggs, three cups sugar, one cup butter, very little soda, flour sufficient not to stick to board.　　　　MRS. E. M'KINSTRY.

JUMBLES, No. 2.

One pound of sugar, one pound of butter, four eggs, one gill of wine, one and one-fourth pounds of flour. Flour your hands very slightly, take a teaspoon of the mixture, roll, and lay in ring. When partly baked, sift powdered sugar over them.
　　　　　　　　　　　　　　　　　　　　　　　　MRS. J. C. M'C.

SUGAR COOKIES.

Two cups sugar, three eggs, one cup butter, two cups sweet milk, two teaspoons of baking powder. Bake in a quick oven.
　　　　　　　　　　　　　　　　　　　　　　　　MRS. A. HAGADORN.

SOFT COOKIES.

Three-fourths pound sugar, one-half pound butter, five eggs, one pound flour, juice and rind of one lemon. Drop spoonful on tins. As soon as warm enough to run, sift sugar over them.
　　　　　　　　　　　　　　　　　　　　　　　　MRS. E. F. S.

TRY PRESERVING YOUR FRUIT WITHOUT HEAT,

BUTTER DROPS.

Two cups butter, two cups sugar, three eggs. Mix stiff, roll thin. S. A. READ.

SUGAR COOKIES, No. 2.

One coffeecup butter, two teacups sugar, one teacup sweet milk, two teaspoons baking powder, two eggs, flavor to taste. Mix very soft, roll thin. O. M. W.

JUMBLES, No. 3.

Two cups sugar, one and one-half cups butter, five cups flour, three eggs, four tablespoons sweet milk, two teaspoons baking powder. MRS. LEWIS CLARK.

CHOCOLATE JUMBLES.

One and one-half teacups white sugar, one-half cup sweet cream, one half cup butter, one cup grated chocolate, one-half teaspoon soda dissolved in cream, one-half teaspoon cream tarter, one egg. Work very stiff with flour; mix chocolate and cream tartar in the flour, roll thin. MRS. B. F. SPRAKER.

COCOANUT PUFFS.

One cup cocoanut, one cup powdered sugar, beaten whites of two eggs, two tablespoons of flour or corn starch; drop on buttered tins, bake quickly. F. M. S.

HICKORY NUT MACAROONS.

One cup sugar, one large or two small eggs, five tablespoons of flour, one cup chopped nuts. Drop from a spoon in buttered tins and bake. MISS M. DUNN.

GINGER SNAPS, No. 1.

Two cups of molasses, one of lard, one tablespoon ginger, one teaspoon salt, two teaspoons soda. Put all together, let boil, stiffen with flour, and roll very thin. MRS. A. HAGADORN.

GINGER SNAPS, No 2.

One quart of molasses, one pound of sugar, one pound of butter, two teaspoons soda, three tablespoons of ginger, two of cloves. Boil molasses, butter, sugar and spices together for ten minutes; when cold add soda, and flour to roll easily. Roll very thin.
M. J. C. M'C.

USING PETTIT'S CIDER AND FRUIT PRESERVATIVE.

GINGER SNAPS, No. 3.

One cup molasses, one-half cup brown sugar, one cup butter, tablespoon ginger, one teaspoon soda. Boil molasses and sugar together, then add butter and ginger. When cool add flour.

MISS MARY WELLS.

LEMON SNAPS.

One large cup of sugar, little more than one-half cup butter, two eggs, two tablespoons boiling water, one-half teaspoon soda, two teaspoons lemon, flour to roll easily. MRS. G. W. GOODRICH.

SNOW BALLS.

One cup powdered sugar, one of thick sweet cream, whites five eggs, two teaspoons baking powder. Bake in gem tins—frost.

MARTHA A. RICE.

WAFERS.

Two cups butter, two cups sugar, two eggs, two cups flour—scant. Do not mix stiff, flavor. Roll very thin. They require very little baking. MRS. J. C. M'C.

SAND TARTS.

One pound flour, one pound sugar, three-fourths pound butter, the white of one egg, and yolks of two. Cream butter, add sugar and beat well, then eggs, then flour, making a stiff dough. Roll very thin and cut into shape, moisten the tops with white of egg, sprinkle with fine sugar, mixed with cinnamon, have ready half a pound almonds, blanched and split; put one or two on each cake, and bake in quick oven. MISS M. M. NELLIS.

TRY PRESERVING YOUR FRUIT WITHOUT HEAT,

FRUITS.

PRESERVED, JELLIED, CANNED AND PICKLED.

In putting up fruits, use granulated, or best white coffee sugar; cook only in porcelain kettle, or bright tin preserving-pan. Let a little hot water stand in glass cans for a short time before putting fruit in.

In the following recipes, where "bowls" are mentioned, use one that will hold one pint and a half.

TO CAN PEACHES.

For each can, allow one heaping bowl of peeled and halved peaches, one-half bowl of sugar and a coffee cup of water. Make a syrup of sugar and water, only boiling just enough to make clear, strain, cool, and pour over the peaches, which have already been put in cans. Have a wooden rack at bottom of large boiler, on which place cans, and fill nearly to the top of cans, with cool water, set on stove and cover. After water has come to a boil, let them remain from ten to twenty minutes, according to ripeness of fruit. Take out, let stand a couple of minutes to settle, fill up with reserved syrup, and put in cans, closing securely. Screw down covers again, when cool, and try by turning upside down before setting away. If the cans leak, the fruit must be heated again.

CANNED PLUMS.

Can them in same manner as laid down for peaches, using same proportions of fruit, sugar and water as above.

FOR RED AND BLACK RASPBERRIES AND BLACKBERRIES.

Take in following proportions: three bowls fruit to one of sugar, and half a bowl water. Put together, set on stove long enough to heat throughout, and boil for not more than five minutes, then can. This quantity fills two cans.

CHERRIES.

To six pounds stoned fruit, add three pounds sugar, and one and a half pints of warm water. Set on stove, let boil thoroughly for five minutes, and can. This should be enough for five cans.

USING PETTIT'S CIDER AND FRUIT PRESERVATIVE.

STRAWBERRIES.

To six lbs. fruit use three lbs. sugar; put in pan alternately, and let stand a few minutes to draw out juice. Heat slowly, taking off when the fruit has boiled not more than five minutes.

CURRANTS AND GOOSEBERRIES.

May be canned in the same manner, and are nice for pies.

PEARS AND QUINCES.

Are canned alike. Pare, halve, core and drop into cold water, until all are ready. To one lb. fruit, take half pound sugar. First cook fruit till tender in water, keeping closely covered, or the fruit will darken; when tender, pour off water, leaving it an inch below surface of fruit; pour in sugar and boil for ten minutes. To pears add slices of lemon, or small pieces of ginger root just before putting into the cans.

SPICED GRAPES.

Press pulp of grapes out of the skins, and put it over to boil, until the seeds are loosened, then pass through a colander to separate them. Put pulp and skins together and weigh them; to five lbs. grapes take two and one-half lbs. brown sugar, one pint vinegar, one heaped teaspoon each of salt, pepper, cloves, cinnamon and allspice. Mix thoroughly, set on range, and boil until they are somewhat thickened, being careful they do not burn. To eat with meats.

CRAB APPLE JELLY.

Take the stems and flower-buds from the apples, cut out spots, and cut in half, if large. Put on range with water enough to come just to top of fruit, cover closely, and cook until it is thoroughly soft. Mash well, and turn into jelly bag, and let drain, from afternoon till next morning, when all that is good will have come through. Measure juice, and to each pint, allow one full pint of sugar; boil the juice briskly for fifteen minutes, and skim, then add the sugar, let it come again to a boil, and skim while boiling, for ten minutes longer; or until, when the drops in falling from the spoon, will jelly on it, before all has dripped away. Turn into tumblers or bowls, cover with some thin fabric to keep flies away, until hardened, which will be in one or two days. Cover top of jelly

---

TRY PRESERVING YOUR FRUIT WITHOUT HEAT,

with letter paper dipped in brandy; and the bowls, glasses, etc., with brown paper dipped in white of eggs, or dissolved gelatine.

QUINCE JELLY.

Cut up the quinces without peeling, using part only, of the seeds. The peelings of those which are to be canned, can also be used for jelly, and a few apples may be added, if desired. Proceed exactly as with the crab-apples.

GRAPE AND PLUM JELLY.

These can be made in same manner, except that they take much less time to cook soft than the others. Any juice which may not drip from the bag over night, will not be clear, or make a clear jelly. This is a much easier way to make jellies, than to squeeze juice through bag while it is hot.

YELLOW TOMATO PRESERVES.

Remove the skins, take half a pound of sugar to one of tomatoes; boil till syrup is thick; before they are quite done, add lemon sliced thin, allowing one to a quart. Put in cans. HETTIE B. B.

PICKLED PLUMS,

For seven pounds of plumbs, take three of sugar, one quart of vinegar, one ounce whole cloves, one ounce stick cinnamon. Boil together sugar, vinegar and spices, throw over the fruit. When cool, strain off the syrup; boil and pour over fruit, repeating again the first day. Let stand three days, drain off, and boil again.

MRS. M'C.

PICKLED PEARS.

Quantity of fruit, sugar, vinegar and spices, same as for plums. Steam pears till tender. Dissolve sugar in vinegar, with spices; let boil and pour on fruit. MRS. OLLIE ABELL.

RIPE CUCUMBER PICKLES.

Soak sliced cucumbers in weak vinegar twenty-four hours. Dry them, make a syrup of two pounds of sugar, one quart vinegar, one of cinnamon buds. Cook until tender. MRS. O. A.

TO STEW CRANBERRIES NICELY.

One cup of sugar, half a cup of water, one and a half of cranberries. Bring sugar and water to boiling, stir in berries, keep stirring till all are burst open. HETTIE B. B.

USING PETTIT'S CIDER AND FRUIT PRESERVATIVE.
F

APPLES STEWED WHOLE.

Pare, and with an apple corer or small knife, extract the core of good, juicy apples; put in a deep dish with just enough water to cover them; put in steamer and steam till tender and clear; take out apples carefully, put in a dish and cover to keep hot. Put the juice in a sauce-pan with a cup of sugar to twelve apples, and boil till like syrup; put in a little mace or whole cloves, ten minutes before removing from the fire. Pour over apples, cover till cold. Eat with cream if desired.   HETTIE B. B.

CURRANT JELLY.

Put currants on the stove in a pan till warmed thoroughly, then squeeze; for each pint of juice, take one pound of sugar; let the juice come to a boil, pour it over the sugar, stir well, and when sugar is dissolved pour into glasses.   MRS. M'C.

SPICED CURRANTS.

To five pounds currants, three pounds sugar, half pint vinegar, one tablespoon each cloves, cinnamon and allspice, tied in a cloth. Boil about 35 minutes.   MRS. OLLIE ABELL.

TUTTI-FRUTTI.

Put in a stone jar three pounds sugar, one pint brandy. Then for each pound of fruit put in, add one pound of sugar. This should be begun with strawberries, and add the various fresh fruits as they come in their season.

TUTTI-FRUTTI, No. 2.

Put in two-gallon jar one quart brandy and three pounds granulated sugar. Then, as various kinds of fruit are obtained, add one pound of sugar to each pound of fruit. Begin with strawberries, cherries stoned, banannas, pineapples cut in pieces, etc. Keep in a cool place, and stir every few days, till the last of the fruit has been added. The quantity of brandy and sugar mentioned at first will bear seven or eight pounds each of fruit and extra sugar. Cover with paper, or transfer to cans or small jars. Use only choice fruit. To serve with cream, freeze with it, or in lemon jelly or pudding sauce.   MRS. N. S. BRUMLEY.

TRY PRESERVING YOUR FRUIT WITHOUT HEAT,

PRESERVED PINEAPPLES.

After paring, cut in pieces in a chopping bowl, leaving out the core or hard part. Chop pretty fine. Then chop the core by itself, strain through a sieve, put together and weigh, allowing three-quarters of a pound of sugar to one of fruit. Boil a few minutes and put in cans.
MRS. S. A. R.

CRANBERRY JELLY.

Put one quart cranberries to boil in one pint cold water. Have ready in a bowl one pint of sugar. When berries are perfectly soft, mash while hot into bowl containing sugar, and stir till dissolved. Pour in mold and set on ice twenty-four hours.
MRS. E. M'K.

CONFECTIONS.

BUTTER SCOTCH.

Two cups molasses, butter size of an egg, one cup of brown sugar, one-third of a cup of vinegar. Boil until it hardens in cold water, and pour in buttered tins.

CHOCOLATE CARAMELS.

Two cups brown sugar, one cup of milk, one cup of molasses, one-quarter of a pound of chocolate, butter size of an egg. Boil until it hardens in cold water, and pour in buttered tins.

CHOCOLATE CREAMS.

Two cups sugar, one-half cup of water. Boil until it strings, put aside to cool, then stir to a thick cream. Flavor with vanilla or lemon, and make into balls. Melt one-half a cake of chocolate, dip the balls in it, and place on buttered plates in a cool place.

CREAM DATES.

Make cream as directed for chocolate creams. Take one-half pound fresh dates, remove stones, and fill centers of dates with cream.

USING PETTIT'S CIDER AND FRUIT PRESERVATIVE.

PICKLES, ETC.

FRENCH CHOW CHOW.

One quart large green cucumbers cut in pieces, one quart very small ones, one quart button onions, one quart green tomatoes sliced and cut in pieces, one large cauliflower cut small, four large peppers cut in coarse bits. Put all in a weak brine, (one cup of salt to a gallon of water,) for twenty-four hours. Scald in same brine and drain. Make a paste of six tablespoons ground mustard, one of tumeric, one cup of flour, one of sugar, two quarts cider vinegar. First moisten the dry materials with a little vinegar, then add the remainder, stirring continually till smooth and thick, then add the pickles. MRS. W. N. S

TOMATO CATSUP.

Cut up and boil the tomatoes till soft, sift them, to one gallon, add one-half teaspoon cayenne pepper, two of black pepper, two of cinnamon, two of cloves, one coffee cup of sugar, one quart vinegar, and boil till thick. E.

CHILI SAUCE.

Six quarts ripe tomatoes cut up and boiled until soft, then run through a colander to take out skins. Add nine peppers and three onions finely chopped, three tablespoons salt, six tablespoons sugar, three of ginger, four of cloves, five of cinnamon, two of allspice, three pints vinegar. Boil till it thickens. Bottle. E.

CRISP CUCUMBER PICKLES.

Cover pickles with a boiling hot brine made in the proportion of one cup of salt to four quarts of water. The next day, or when cold, turn off brine and boil again, turning on hot. Repeat eight or nine times, after which drain till dry. Take vinegar enough to cover. Spice to taste, or get mixed spices. Five cents' worth is enough for a two-gallon jar. Boil spice in vinegar and pour on hot. MRS. S. A. R.

GREEN TOMATO SAUCE.

One peck tomatoes, twelve onions chopped fine, half a cup of salt, one-half cup ground mustard, one ounce ground ginger, one-half cup white mustard seed, one-fourth pound black pepper. Put

TRY PRESERVING YOUR FRUIT WITHOUT HEAT,

tomatoes, onions and spices in alternate layers in a kettle, cover with vinegar, add one pound brown sugar, and stew for two hours.

MRS. M. F. S.

MIXED PICKLES.

One half peck small cucumbers, one pint nasturtiums, one quart string beans, one quart onions, four carrots cut in pieces, two cauliflowers, two ounces white mustard seed, one ounce black, one-half pint salt, one-fourth pound mustard, mixed with one-fourth bottle table oil, three cents worth celery seed. Mix all well together; put in a stone jar; scald vinegar enough to cover them; add a little sugar.

MRS. M A. F.

LILLY PICKLE.

Slice green tomatoes and onions very thin; put in stone jar a layer of tomatoes two inches thick, then a single layer of onions; proceed in this way until jar is full, then for a two gallon jar, take one pint salt, and enough water to cover the tomatoes, which must stand over night. In the morning, drain off the brine carefully; put in jar and mix with pickle, one-half cup white mustard seed, two tablespoons peppercorns, two tablespoons dry mustard, first mixed with a little vinegar, and enough more vinegar to cover. Stand jar in pot of boiling water, for about an hour; and when all has cooled, remove pickle to smaller jars, and tie up closely.

MRS. E. F. S.

SPICED VINEGAR FOR PICKLES.

To five quarts vinegar, one and three-fourths pounds brown sugar, one fourth pound white mustard seed, one-fourth bottle table mustard, one-fourth pound white ginger, two ounces each, ground pepper and turmeric, one-half ounce each, nutmeg, ground all-spice, mace, cloves and celery seed. Pound these all well before putting into the vinegar; add one-fourth pound scraped horse-radish, one large sliced lemon, one half dozen small onions scalded in brine, and laid in salt for a day. Pickles should lie in plain vinegar for two weeks before putting them in this mixture.

USING PETTIT'S CIDER AND FRUIT PRESERVATIVE.

BEVERAGES.

COFFEE.

For six people, take a coffeecup of ground coffee, put in half an egg, stir well, add one pint cold water, and stir again. Set coffee pot on cool part of stove, and let it come slowly to a boil; stir down and fill in desired quantity of boiling water, let stand to boil a few minutes, and put to one side, until ready to take to table. It should not stand long. Serve, if possible, with a large teaspoon of whipped cream on top of each cup.

ICED TEA.

The usual allowance is one teaspoon of tea leaves, and a little more than one cup water to each person. For iced tea, make in the morning a stronger tea than usual, sweeten and set in cold place, until wanted. Pour into goblets, half filled with pieces of ice.

CHOCOLATE.

Soak two squares of Baker's chocolate, (without cutting fine,) in one-half cup water, with two even tablespoons sugar for two hours, on back of range, when it will be reduced to paste. Have one quart milk boiling in double boiler, pour in the chocolate, and cook ten minutes, stirring constantly. Serve with whipped cream.

RASPBERRY SHRUB.

For three quarts ripe berries, take one quart good vinegar, put together and let stand twenty-four hours, then strain, and add to each pint of juice one pound of white sugar. Boil the whole together, half an hour, skim and bottle.

GRAPE WINE.

To every gallon of well bruised grapes, add one gallon of water; let stand one week, then add three pounds sugar to every gallon of wine; let it stand for three months, draw off and bottle.

ELDER-FLOWER CORDIAL.

Take three gallons water, nine pounds white sugar. Let this boil, add the white of one egg, well beaten, skim, and add one

---

TRY PRESERVING YOUR FRUIT WITHOUT HEAT,

quart elder-flowers (good measure) to the boiling mixture. Stir and remove from fire, and put in a large jar; when cool, add three tablesoooons lemon juice, and one yeast cake, stirring well. After six days, add three pounds of seedless raisins, or others if these cannot be procured. Put in a large jug, corking loosely at first; let stand for six months, then rack off and bottle.

A FEW USEFUL HINTS.

FOR MILDEW OR FRUIT STAINS.

One half pound chloride of lime, one-fourth pound sal soda; put the lime in a jar with one pint water, and let it stand over night; next morning add the soda and three quarts water; stir well, let it settle and bottle it. Stains and mildew will soon disappear from clothes soaked in it, but should not be allowed to stand more then fifteen minutes. Then wash out thoroughly and rinse.

TO WASH BLANKETS.

Fold the blankets and lay in large tub or bathing tub. Pour plenty of strong warm borax water, with a little white soap dissolved in it, over the blankets, enough to cover them. Turn the blankets occasionally, keeping them folded, however, and let them soak several hours. Then rinse in warm water and put through the wringer. This method saves shrinkage and keeps them soft.

MRS. H. D. WALKER.

CHILBLAINS. A SURE RELIEF.

One pint of strong vinegar, a lump of alum as big as a butternut, one teaspoon saltpetre. Set on the stove until hot and dissolved. Bathe the feet two or three times in this mixture, using it *hot* during the afternoon and evening. When retiring, use for fifteen minutes and rub the feet a long time with the hand.

MRS. H P. W.

USING PETTIT'S CIDER AND FRUIT PRESERVATIVE.

TO REMOVE RUST FROM STEEL.

Cover the steel with sweet oil. well rubbed on. Forty-eight hours after rub it well with unslacked lime, finely powdered, until all the rust disappears.

TO REMOVE SUN BURN.

One pint simple tincture of benzoine and sixteen parts of distilled water. Bath the skin with this twice a day.

TO DESTROY WATER BUGS.

Clean the sink and dry it well at night. Sprinkle powdered borax about the water pipes.

AN EXCELLENT DEODORIZER.

To purify a sick room, put one tablespoonful of bromo chloralum to eight of soft water. Dip clothes in and hang up. This will also purify the breath which is offensive from decayed teeth, rinsing the mouth several times a day.

FROST ON WINDOWS.

Windows may be kept free from frost by rubbing the glass with a cloth wet with alcohol.

TO CLEAN FEATHERS.

Cover the feathers with a paste made of pipe clay and water. Rub them one way only. When quite dry, shake off the powder and curl them with a knife. Grebe feathers may be washed with white soap and soft water.

CAMPHOR ICE.

One ounce of lard, one ounce of spermaceti, one ounce of camphor, one ounce of almond oil, one-half cake of white wax, melted together.

TOOTH POWDER.

Equal parts of gum of myrrh, prepared chalk, orris root and Peruvian bark, pulverized together and well mixed.

TO RESTORE COLOR.

Colors destroyed by acids may be restored by applying ammonia ; after it chloroform.

TRY PRESERVING YOUR FRUIT WITHOUT HEAT,

TO RAISE THE PILE OF VELVET.

Hold over boiling hot steam, wrong side of velvet to the steam. Then pass the back of the velvet over a hot sad iron.

TO KEEP FURS FROM MOTH.

Whip them well, tie them in linen bags, put into the boxes, then wrap closely in newspapers, tie or seal securely. No aromatics are needed.

WELSH RAREBIT.

One-fourth pound rich cream cheese, one-fourth cup cream or milk, one teaspoonful mustard, one-half teaspoonful salt, a few grains of cayenne, one egg, one teaspoonful butter, four slices toast. Break the cheese in small pieces, or, if hard, grate it. Put it, with the milk, in a double boiler. Toast the bread and keep it hot. Mix the mustard, salt and pepper, add the egg and beat well. When the cheese is melted stir in the egg and butter and cook two minutes, or until it thickens a little, but do not let it curdle. Pour it over the toast. Many use ale instead of cream.

BOSTON COOK BOOK.

USING PETTIT'S CIDER AND FRUIT PRESERVATIVE.

Preserve Your Fruit Without Heat!

—: BY USING :—

PETTIT'S
CIDER and FRUIT
PRESERVATIVE.

This article has been upon the market for several years, giving in each and every case perfect satisfaction. It having been extensively used, a very large number of testimonials could be recorded here, but we believe it unnecessary, preferring to allow it to be sold upon its merit.

This article is harmless. It will keep cider, fruit, etc., perfectly. Give it a trial and enjoy the great relief of putting up fruit without heat.

PRICE, 40 CENTS PER BOX.

Ask your druggist or grocer for it. If you cannot find it in your place we will send it to any address on receipt of price. Complete directions in each box.

PETTIT MFG. CO.,
CANAJOHARIE, N. Y.

SPECIAL SALE
—>OF<—
SEAL GARMENTS.

COTTRELL & LEONARD,
ALBANY,

are making a Special Sale of Seal Sacques, Wraps, Jackets, &c., previous to inventory, and are offering First Quality Seal Goods at prices which cannot be made next season. Seal will be higher, and it will pay to buy a Garment, Cap or Gloves now, even for next year's use.

☞ PLUSH SACKS AND WRAPS.

472 and 474 Broadway,
ALBANY, N. Y.

A BEAR STANDS BY THE DOOR.

ALBANY

Evening Journal

—: WILL BE :—

⇒DELIVERED TO YOUR HOUSE⇐

Every Evening

—: FOR :—

18 CENTS PER WEEK.

If you cannot get it of your news dealer, address

THE JOURNAL CO.,
ALBANY, N. Y.

STONE & SHANKS,
56 North Pearl St.,
ALBANY, N. Y.

Will hold during January and February a special sale of

Fine Lace Curtains.

This sale will include their entire line of novelties in

SASH CURTAINS,

And prices will be named to make the sale specially attractive.

Fifty-Two "Cook" Books,

Giving a correct and graphic description of local events as they occur.

AT ONLY $1.50.

The above refers to a year's subscription to

The Wide Awake Courier,

CANAJOHARIE, N. Y.,

Which is the Breeziest, Brightest and Best Weekly Paper in the Mohawk Valley.

Editor and Proprietor, WILLET F. COOK.

C. STICHT,

DEALER IN

Boots, Shoes and Rubbers.

HOUSE ESTABLISHED 1850.

CANAJOHARIE, N. Y.

HATTERS'.

The Oldest and Largest Clothing Emporium in Central New York.

DEALERS IN

∴ Ready-Made Clothing, ∴

HATS, CAPS AND GENTS' FURNISHING GOODS.

CUSTOM WORK A SPECIALTY.

FOR

Carpets,

• Rugs, •

• Mats and •

• Mattings,

GO TO

A. B. VAN GAASBEEK & CO.

69 North Pearl St.,

ALBANY, N. Y.

The Greatest Triumph of the Age
IN MEDICINE.

Pettit's Little Liver Pills.

A CERTAIN CURE FOR

Constipation, Head Ache, Liver Complaint,

DYSPEPSIA AND BILIOUSNESS.

Many persons, particularly ladies, dislike to take Pills; but there are numerous reasons why the pill form of administering medicine is preferable. With a view to meet this objection as far as possible, we have compounded PETTIT'S LITTLE LIVER PILLS of the most highly concentrated medicinal roots, and they are therefore so small that they can be easily taken; and, being sugar coated, are rendered tasteless. We feel sure a trial will convince you that they are far superior to any other in the market. If your druggist does not keep them, send us 25 cents and we will send you a box by mail.

PETTIT MFG. CO.,
CANAJOHARIE, N. Y.

Custom's Injuries.

Described by a Noted London Dentist.

37 High Holborn,
London. W. C.

GENTLEMEN: I consider the bristle tooth brush has to answer in no little measure for the receding gums around the necks of the teeth so constantly brought to our notice. After thoroughly testing the

"I TANT WEAD IT. TAN OO?"

I have no hesitation in saying that *any one who uses it for one week will never go back to the old bristle brush with its attendant miseries of Loose Bristles and Constantly Wounded Gums.*

Faithfully yours,
J. SHIPLEY SLIPPER, Dental Surgeon.

ITS ECONOMY.

Holder (imperishable), 35 cents. Polishers only need be renewed; 18 (boxed), 25 cents. At dealers, or mailed.

THE HORSEY MFG. CO,
UTICA, N. Y.

JOHN G. MYERS,

39 and 41 North Pearl Street,

ALBANY, N. Y.

DRY GOODS.

J. C. BEACH,
— MANUFACTURER OF —
Champagne-Cider,
BOILED CIDER,
— AND —
PURE CIDER VINEGAR.
Russet Cider in Bottles a Specialty.

PALATINE BRIDGE, N. Y.

ANDREW DUNN & SON,
WHOLESALE AND RETAIL
JEWELERS,
AND IMPORTERS OF
Diamonds AND Artistic Novelties.

The largest stock in the Mohawk Valley of **Diamonds, Jewelry Watches and Clocks, Bronzes, and Novelties and Objects D'Art. Badges, Society Pins, and Prizes of all kinds.**

For ingenuity of composition, delicacy of chasing, gracefulness and good taste of the details, our goods are unexcelled.

REPAIRING A SPECIALTY.

ANDREW DUNN & SON, Fort Plain, N. Y.

TO OBTAIN THE GREATEST SUCCESS

with the valuable recipes contained in this book, you should use the

ACME BAKING POWDER,

WHICH IS ABSOLUTELY

PURE and HEALTHFUL.

If your Grocer does not keep it send orders to

KIRBY & DIEFENDORF,

CANAJOHARIE, N. Y.,

owners of this celebrated brand.

☞ Mail orders promptly attended to.

☞ Discount to the trade on application.

KIRBY & DIEFENDORF,
36 Church Street,   CANAJOHARIE, N. Y.

Ask Your Druggist for

HANSON'S
Magic Corn Salve.

If he does not keep it, do not let him convince you that some imitation is just as good. Send by mail to

W. T. HANSON & CO.,
SCHENECTADY, N. Y.

Price, 15 and 25 Cents.

HANSON'S MAGIC CORN SALVE is recommended by 10,000 of the principal Druggists in the U. S. and Canada.

Office of WAGNER PALACE CAR CO.
Opposite Grand Central Depot.
General Superintendent's Office,
NEW YORK, June 29, 1887.

C. D. FLAGG,
General Sup't.
W. T. HANSON & Co., Schenectady, N. Y.

Dear Sirs:—The "Magic Corn Salve" came duly to hand; I immediately gave it a trial, and it affords me much pleasure to say that the results were highly satisfactory. My feet have not for years been in as good condition as they are at present. The remedy is a good one and all who are troubled with corns should use it. Yours truly,
C. D. FLAGG, Gen'l Sup't.

Everybody Reads It!

$4.00 Per Year.

ADDRESS

Publisher Judge,

NEW YORK.

—USE—

BELLINGER & DYGERT'S

Strictly Pure Baking Powder.

It is free from Alum, Lime, Ammonia, Terra Alba, or any adulteration whatever. Contains strictly pure Grape Cream Tartar and Natrona Bi-Carbonate Soda, and is the most reliable and most economical Baking Powder on the market.

MANUFACTURED BY

BELLINGER & DYGERT,

Wholesale and Retail Druggists,

52 Church Street, - CANAJOHARIE, N. Y.

CHARLES W. SCHARFF,

Sole Agent for the

CELEBRATED

"Carton" and "Pease" Furnaces,

CANAJOHARIE, N. Y.

A. E. TANNER,
HARDWARE.
DOCKASH AND MYSTIC RANGES,

ALSO,

Monitor and Crown Oil Stoves,

CANAJOHARIE, N. Y.

DANIEL SPRAKER, Jr.,
General Fire and Life Insurance Agent.

OFFICES AT

CANAJOHARIE and SPRAKERS, N. Y.

ESTABLISHED 1868.   INCORPORATED 1882.

THE LARGEST AND MOST COMPLETE CANNED GOODS PACKING ESTABLISHMENT IN THE WORLD.

CURTICE BROTHERS CO.,
ROCHESTER, N. Y.

PRESERVERS AND PACKERS of extra quality **Canned Fruits, Vegetables, Meats,** and other TABLE DELICACIES.

These goods are for sale by first-class grocers generally. If your grocer does not keep them, send direct for priced catalogue.

If you want the

❖ BEST HAM ❖

in the market, buy

CLARK & WOOD'S

STAR BRAND.

Ask your Grocer for them. Cured by

CLARK & WOOD,

FORT PLAIN, N. Y.

P. J. McMANUS.   P. W. O'REILLY.

McMANUS & O'REILLY,

SUCCESSORS TO **JOHNSTON & REILLY,**

Dry Goods,

59 & 61 North Pearl St.,

ALBANY, N. Y.

FREAR'S TROY BAZAAR,

Employing over 300 people and containing a stock of Staple and Fancy Dry Goods aggregating in value over $500,000, comprising the latest choice styles, offers shoppers the very best facilities, and is pronounced by all

THE LEADING
Dry Goods House
OF NORTHERN NEW YORK.

Wm. H. Frear, purchasing his goods direct from the manufacturers, and paying spot cash, can afford to, and does sell his goods at lower prices than any other retail merchant in the State. The best place to trade is at

FREAR'S TROY BAZAAR.

LEWIS S. DAVIS,
CANAJOHARIE, N. Y.
—DEALER IN—
Stoves, Hardware, Iron, Steel, Etc.,
—AND IN—
THE NEW BEAUTY OIL STOVE.
LATEST AND BEST.   FREE FROM ALL ODORS.

☞ Should always be used to obtain best results from recipes given in this book. ☜

FRANK SHUBERT,
CANAJOHARIE, N. Y.
— DEALER IN—
Boots, Shoes and Rubbers.
☞ **FINE GOODS OF ALL KINDS A SPECIALTY.** ☜

JOHN A. ZOLLER.   HENRY ZOLLER.

JOHN A. ZOLLER & BRO.,
—DEALERS IN ALL KINDS OF—
Lumber, Shingles, Lath, Etc.
—MANUFACTURERS OF—
SASH, DOORS AND BLINDS.

Mouldings and Turned Work of all kinds.

Window and Door Frames made to order.

All kinds of Planing, Scroll and other Sawing.

ADJOINING SPRING AND AXLE WORKS,

FORT PLAIN, N. Y.

Don't Fail to see the Unsurpassed **BOARDMAN & GRAY PIANOS**

ALSO AGENTS FOR THE POPULAR
SCHUBERT PIANO.

From $225 Upwards.

FACTORY AND WAREROOMS,
543 to 549 Broadway, over N. Y. C. RR.
Arcade, ALBANY, N. Y.

ESTABLISHED 1837. Sold by
F. C. LEPPERT,
Canajoharie, N. Y.

BEFORE YOU BUY. [Send for Catalogue.]

J. L. EARLL.   F. H. LATIMORE.

Household Art Rooms,

173 GENESEE STREET, UP STAIRS.

Expert Upholsterers and Decorators.

MAKE FROM SPECIAL DESIGNS

Draperies,   **Portieres,**

Upholstered and Cabinet Furniture,

Ornamental Wood,

Metal and Glass Work.

Their collection of **Wall Papers** embraces the most effective productions of American and foreign manufacturers, while the most recent ideas of ceiling decoration are expressed in their original sketches.

With the working details under the personal direction of F. H. Latimore, they invite orders for the decoration of single rooms or entire houses.

PATENT
Reliance and Sanitary Refrigerators,

—MANUFACTURED BY—

The Sweet Refrigerator Company,

CANAJOHARIE, N. Y.

They have been in use several years, and are therefore known to possess the following qualities:

1st. Perfectly dry air.
2d. Economy in the consumption of ice.
3d. Preservation of contents longer and in better condition than any other refrigerator in the market.
4th. No zinc or other metal lining to corrode.
5th. Easy to keep clean.
6th. Twenty-five per cent. more inside space than any other refrigerator with the same outside measurements.
7th. Do not require broken ice.
8th. Made of the best material.
9th. All sizes and forms, for dwellings, hotels, stores, restaurants, markets.
10th. Entire freedom from all moisture.

Has been awarded medal for highest merits at the American Institute Fair. For prices and further particulars write to

THE SWEET REFRIGERATOR CO.
CANAJOHARIE, N. Y.

www.ingramcontent.com/pod-product-compliance
Lightning Source LLC
Chambersburg PA
CBHW020154170426
43199CB00010B/1033